THE FUR HUNTERS

OF THE FAR WEST;

A NARRATIVE OF

ADVENTURES IN THE OREGON AND
ROCKY MOUNTAINS.

BY ALEXANDER ROSS,

AUTHOR OF "ADVENTURES OF THE FIRST SETTLERS ON THE OREGON OR
COLUMBIA RIVER."

IN TWO VOLUMES.

VOL. II.

LONDON:
SMITH, ELDER AND CO., 65, CORNHILL.
1855.

LONDON:
WOODFALL AND KINDER,
ANGEL COURT, SKINNER STREET.

This scarce antiquarian book is included in our special *Legacy Reprint Series*. In the interest of creating a more extensive selection of rare historical book reprints, we have chosen to reproduce this title even though it may possibly have occasional imperfections such as missing and blurred pages, missing text, poor pictures, markings, dark backgrounds and other reproduction issues beyond our control. Because this work is culturally important, we have made it available as a part of our commitment to protecting, preserving and promoting the world's literature. Thank you for your understanding.

Ford & West Lith.

Alexander Ross

Published by Smith Elder & Co Cornhill 1855

CONTENTS OF VOL. II.

CHAPTER X.

The Snake country—M'Donald's trip—Arrival of Mr. Dease—Leave Fort Nez Percés—Reach the Rocky Mountains—Governor Simpson's communication—M'Donald's return—Preparations for the Snake country—Cross purposes—Disappointments—Leave Spokane House—The medley—History of the fifty-five—General remarks—Departure of the expedition—Game scarce—Mr. Howe in 1810—Iroquois singing hymns—Their plans—New regulations—Comparison between large and small rifles—Hunting regulations—Delegates appointed—Hell's Gates—Remarks—Difficulties—New route—Wild horses—Game—Piegans—Iroquois desert—A hard ride—The deserters surprised—Six Nez Percés—Rams' horns a curiosity—Indian legend—Gloomy accounts of the road. The Valley of Troubles—Parties in search of a pass—Prospects more and more gloomy—The discovering party—Wandering Snakes—Their dress—Alarm—The party under arms—Nez Percés—Surmises—Iroquois caught in their own trap—Indian reports—Nez Percés off—Conduct of the Iroquois—The discovering party arrive—Dine on the Snow—

Depth of snow in the mountain—Distance—A council held—Discouraging circumstances—Disaffection—The camp in disorder—John Grey the ringleader—His plots counteracted—The crisis—A bold undertaking—Road-making—Men and horses—Extraordinary efforts—A novel sight—Depth of snow—Try it again—Plans for making the road changed—Persisted in—Completed—Anxieties—Extreme point of Flathead River—Its length—Leave the Valley of Troubles—Source of the Missouri River—Cross the mountain—The effect of perseverance . . Page 1

CHAPTER XI.

Camp regulations—Beaver—Tracks of enemies—Hot spring—Snow-storm—Narrow escape—Missouri—Lewis and Clarke's track—Successful trapping—Dangerous passes—The battle—Seven trappers killed—Piegans roasted—Hardihood—Iroquois shot—Horrid cruelties—Revenge—Salmon River—Herds of buffalo—Canoe Point—Young grass—War roads—Night-watch—Heedless trappers—Martin and his horses—Scouting parties—Discouraging prospects—Hackana in favour—New prospects—Dangerous roads—Disappointments—Effect—Hackana in disgrace—A horse killed—The alarm—Escape of a child—Rock-turn-again—Twelve days' experience—Return to Canoe Point—The beaver cache—Swimming—Salmon River—Hot springs—Enemies appear—Pursuit—Buffalo—Forlorn trappers—Piegan war-party—Fruitless search—The mistake—Two men robbed—Looking the wrong way—Subterraneous river—A four days' ramble—Cold—Horses die—Division of the party—River Malade—Alarm—War-party—A night's dancing—Indian cunning—A horse killed—Scalps—Trapping difficulties—Watch—Perverse trappers—The alarm—Paying too dear for a drink of cold water—A horse killed—A scamper—Piegans again—Chief's declaration—New road—Frightful passes—Hard shifts—Reid's River—Dismal prospects—Disaffected people—A stand still—Two Bannatees—Their story—Three Bannatees—Their fears . 49

CHAPTER XII.

A calm after a storm—Gloomy aspect—Cheering prospects—Plenty, and smiling countenances—Pee-eye-em and suite—His manner—Cayouse plenipotentiaries—The peace—A ride round the great Snake camp—The council—Ceremony of smoking—More honour than comfort—A supperless night—Peace concluded—Escort—Barter with the Snakes—The three rivers described—Beaver—Division of the party—Horse-racing—An Iroquois outwitted—The trick—Indians at home—Awkward position of the whites—Ama-ketsa—The crafty chief—Encamp in a wrong place—Excursion round the camp—Salmon—War-are-reekas—Their character—The trap quarrel—Conduct of the whites—Seize ten of the Snake horses—Rogues surprised—Stratagem—A camp cleared—The pipe stem—Stolen traps restored—Return of good feelings—Raise camp—Waterfalls—Salmon-fishery—News of the Iroquois—Point Turnagain—Comparison of distances—Natural bridge—Subterraneous river—Hot and cold springs—Valley of lightning—Thunder—Rivière aux Malades—Poisonous beaver—A horse drowned—Snake surprised—Bannatees in winter—Hazardous travelling—Mount Simpson—The Governor's punch-bowl—Source of Salmon River—Conjectures—The wounded pheasant—Bear River—A bear hunt—The bear and the beaver—The last shift—A horse drowned—Hard work and little progress—Canoe Point again—Disabled horses—Narrow escape—A man died—Buffalo plenty—The wounded bull—Habits of the buffalo—Iroquois arrive—Their story—Their conduct—American trappers.
Page 90

CHAPTER XIII.

Report—Enemies in sight—The agreeable mistake—The ten Nez Percés—Their story—Suspicious defile—Reconnoitring party—Enemies discovered—The pursuit—A hard ride—The hiding-place—Gathering the spoil—The peace-offering—Suspicious party—Anxieties of the whites—The surprise—The stolen horses—The thieves caught—Indians mute—Nez Percés reproved—Thieves in custody—Return to camp—The court-martial—Wild fowl—Sporting—Hard shooting—World of game—The mourning scene—The snowy mountain—Change of scenery—Valley of Troubles again—Ice and snow—Cold travelling—Hell's Gates—A horse drowned—Arrive at Flathead house—Fruits of the expedition—Remarks—Yankee enterprise—New plan proposed—The men—Contemplated results—Depôt for the returns—Wants created—Inland position—Speculation—Sketch of the Snake people—Position of the Snakes—Their courage—Snake language . . . . Page 131

CHAPTER XIV.

Dawn of education on the Oregon—Speech of a Kootanais chief—The farewell—Juvenile adventurers—Result—Flathead River—The Forks—Interview—Party set out for the Rocky Mountains—Parting scene—Facilities—Bold undertaking—View of the subject—Kettle Falls—Fort Colville—Remarks—Gloomy place—Petit Dalles—Some account of the place—Islands—A boat in jeopardy—Kootanais River—Stony barrier—Desolation—No Indians—No animals—First lake—Extent—Scenery—The wounded Indian—Jealousy in the wilderness—New-fashioned canoes—Link between the lakes—Upper lake—Sudden appearance of an Indian—Chief of the Sinatcheggs—His story—Some account of his country and people—The deception—Length of upper lake—Some account of the country—The child—Peace-offering—The wretched flock—Gloomy aspect—Perilous navigation—The ideal city—M'Kenzie's River—Dalles des Morts—Seat of desolation—Natural curiosity—Moisture—Castle-rock ores—Transparent substances—A man in a gold mine—Ross's River—Cataract creeks—The circus—Diamond creek—Brilliant objects—Beaver islands—M'Millan's River—Landscape in confusion—Belle Vue point—Deceitful windings—The steersman's warning—Canoe River—Northernmost point of Columbia—Portage River—Main branch—Length of north branch—Land on Portage point—Columbia voyage concluded . . . 156

CHAPTER XV.

Portage Point—Wild scenery—Forbidding prospect—The five tribes—Begin the portage—The walking-stick Journal—Hard day's work—Luxuries of the evening camp—Road described—Leave Portage River—Scenery—Portage Valley—Climbing the Grand Côte—Size of the timber—Encampment—Night scene—Punch-bowl Lake—Sister Creeks—Farewell to Columbia—Avalanches—Devastation—Giant of the rocks—Horses arrive—Road obstructions—The Hole—Athabasca—Length of portage—East side scenery—First establishment—North-westers and bark canoes—Jasper's house—Lapensie's grave—Solitary travelling—Fort Assiniboine—Exchange horses for canoes—The new road—Sturgeon River—The party described—Garments—Arrive at Fort Edmonton—Indians—Trade—A ball—Offensive dogs—Saskatchewan boats—Charming scenery—Fort Carlton—Hostile Indians—Agriculture—The swampy country—Crees—Fort Cumberland—Sturgeon—Trade—Gardens—The sun-dial—Domestic cattle—Lake Bourbon—Arctic land expedition—Franklin and Richardson—The country of frogs and mosquitoes—Grand rapid—Miskagoes—Winipeg—Mossy Point—Arrive at Norway House—Migratory habits of the warlike tribes of the plains—Views of the introduction of agriculture—Mr. Leith's bequest . Page 188

CHAPTER XVI.

Nelson River—Route to York Factory—Norway House—Climate—Great rendezvous—Governor Simpson—Annual Councils—The fur trade—Remarks on the present system—The Governor's unlimited power—General remarks—My own final arrangements—Retiring servants—Leave Norway House—Qualities of our boat's crew—Physical deformities—A canoe hero—Account of his life—The voyageur's paradise—More words than work—Gloomy prospects—Dreary shore—Useless hands—Spider Islands—Pop-

rally all on credit. With this number I made preparations for setting out on my expedition.

On assembling my people, I smiled at the medley, the variety of accents, of dresses, habits, and ideas; but, above all, at the confusion of languages in our camp: there were two Americans, seventeen Canadians, five half-breeds from the east side of the mountains, twelve Iroquois, two Abinakee Indians from Lower Canada, two natives from Lake Nipisingue, one Soulteaux from Lake Huron, two Crees from Athabasca, one Chinook, two Spokanes, two Kouttanais, three Flat-heads, two Callispellums, one Palooche, and one Snake slave! Five of the Canadians were above sixty years of age, and two were on the wrong side of seventy. The Iroquois were good hunters, but plotting and faithless. From five to ten of the more trusty and resolute would always be required as a guard on the camp and horses, and could therefore be but seldom employed in trapping beaver; and as for the nineteen natives, they were only of use as far as numbers went, or in taking care of our horses: in these respects, however, they proved very serviceable. So that upon the whole, I could scarcely count on more than twenty trappers at any time.

One-half, perhaps two-thirds, of the people I had under my command were more expert at the bow and arrow than at the use of the beaver trap; more accustomed to indolence and free-will than to subordination.

In summing up, however, we must not forget that twenty-five of the party were married, and several of the youngsters carried guns; so that in our camp there were, exclusive of the men, twenty-five women and sixty-four children. The rest of the equipment consisted of seventy-five guns, a brass three-pounder, 212 beaver-traps, and 392 horses, together with a good stock of powder and ball, and some trading articles. I now observed to my men, that the journey would be long, and not at all times, perhaps, exempt from danger; but that we might, with industry and perseverance, anticipate a successful trip. Yet, if there were any among the party who preferred remaining at home to going on the journey, the choice was now offered them: this I stated as a bar to grumbling on the journey; but the whole, with one voice, exclaimed, "We prefer going." This point being settled, I next warned them that our safety and success would very much depend upon our unanimity and care; and that all would be little enough to guard against surprise and preserve our horses, on which the success of the undertaking depended. Hence, I said, a night-watch would be established and enforced rigidly, during the journey, upon every one in turn. This also met their approbation.

In the days of the north-west, the council of Fort William did everything that could be done to render the trapping system in the Snake country, during M'Kenzie's time, as efficient as possible; but their instructions had to travel 3,000 miles, and to pass through the hands of many subordinates, each of whom, according to the nature of things in this country, had a voice, which influenced the final arrangement, and not unfrequently stripped it of its usefulness! And the same remarks apply in reference to the Hudson's Bay Company, for the council of York Factory is as far removed from the scene of action as the council of Fort William was. M'Kenzie had to combat these evils; so had his successors: but all to little purpose; for the system, instead of improving by experience, is getting worse every day.

The party being now ready, we left the Flatheads, and proceeded on our journey. By starting in the depth of winter, less difficulty was experienced in providing for so many people. Our camp, with all its defects, appeared at a little distance somewhat formidable; as the whole cavalcade, when in marching order, extended a line of a mile or more in length. Having made about eight miles, and killing only one deer—for we had to depend upon our guns for our suppers,—that small animal proved but a slender repast for 137 hungry mouths. We encamped at a place called Prairie de Chevaux, and next day at Prairie de Carnass; here our hunters had a little better luck, killing six deer, so we had a better supper: and we required it, for we had passed two days on only one light meal.

The day following we passed the crossing-place,

where I picked up several pieces of the best iron ore I had seen in the country; at a short distance from that are the Forks. Here we left the main branch of the Flat-head River, where it makes a quick bend to N.W., to the lake of that name. Then following up what is called Jacques Fork, we encamped at Rivière aux Marons, or Wild Horse River. Our travelling went on but slowly, owing to the scarcity of provisions; for we had nothing with us. In the course of this day's travel, we made a halt, and smoked our pipes at a spot on which some faint traces of civilisation were to be seen. A Mr. Howes, an enterprising individual belonging to the Hudson's Bay Company, established himself here in 1810; but after passing part of the winter, he crossed the mountains again, and never returned. I believe this is the first and only instance in which any of the servants of that Company had penetrated so far to the west, prior to the country falling into their own hands in 1821.

Soon after encamping, the Iroquois began to sing hymns: as soon as I heard that, I doubled the watch, and gave strict orders to observe their motions, as the singing of sacred music by these hypocritical wretches is a sure sign of disaffection. As I expected, early next morning, I found the Iroquois in a body, with old Pierre and John Grey at their head, standing at my tent-door. Knowing their character, this did not surprise me. I was, however, anxious to know the cause, and addressed myself, as a matter of course, to the head man. "What now, Pierre?" I asked. "Oh, nothing," replied he; "the Iroquois merely wish to see their accounts." This being a reasonable demand, although somewhat out of place, I of course complied with it; although I well knew that such a request was but the introduction to some other more unreasonable demand, for they had all of them seen their accounts before starting: but this is the way they generally introduce all subjects. After explaining their accounts, I asked them their motives, as this was neither the time nor the place to be inquiring about accounts, nor discussing arrangements. After several remarks, Pierre observed, "Our debts are heavy, and we are never able to reduce them in a large party; allow us to go off by ourselves, and we shall do much better." I reminded them of their conduct when left by M'Kenzie at the river Skamnaugh, and of course resisted their intention; pointing out to them the consequences; stating that the party was already too small, and that a further division would put an end to the expedition altogether. "Why," continued I, "did you not express your wishes before starting, when I offered you either to come or to remain? It is now no longer time, and I hope such a request will not be made again. The Company place great confidence in your exertions, and I shall do everything in my power to make your undertaking comfortable and profitable." With these assurances they seemed satisfied, and we proceeded.

The Iroquois, however, lagged behind, and, arriving some time after we had put up, encamped on one side. This being an unusual step, I suspected all was not right, and that they were still bent on playing us a trick. I, therefore, sent for Pierre, and explained matters fully to him; when I learned for the first time from Pierre that Grey was a plotting busy-body. Confidence was after a time restored, and the Iroquois reconciled once more. In consequence of deep snows and bad weather, we remained for several days in the same encampment. Here I assembled the people, and made some new regulations.

I observed to them that there appeared to be a great and unnecessary waste of ammunition in the camp; that hitherto, while the party were travelling, half of the people—the ignorant as well as the experienced hunters—were occupied in pursuit of game, by which the animals were more frequently frightened than killed, the duties of the journey and camp both neglected, and provisions were scarce: a change of system was, therefore, necessary. To this end it was settled—that four hunters, in turn, should precede the camp daily, and all the rest attend to other duties; and it was anticipated that we should be always better supplied with provisions, other duties would be better attended to, and not a third of the ammunition spent.

In observing the effect produced by guns of different calibres, it was found that the **rifles of small bore**, taking from 60 to 70 balls to the pound, very frequently did not kill, although they might hit; while rifles taking from 30 to 40 to the pound seldom missed killing on the spot. The former out of twenty shots seldom kills more than seven or eight animals; whereas of the latter, if twenty shots are fired, fifteen are generally deadly. It was, therefore, settled that the rifles of larger calibre should be used in all places where **animals** proved scarce.

Our party consisted of four classes of people, differing in almost everything but the **human** form—Canadians, half-breeds, Iroquois, and natives of different nations. It was agreed, with the consent of all, that I should appoint the person of most influence in each party as a head over the rest. This arrangement would relieve me of much trouble, and promised to work well. In all difficult cases I was to call these headmen together, to hold a council, so that things might go on smoothly.

From Rivière au Marons we raised camp, and proceeded on our journey up what is called the valley of Raucin au Mer, or Spetlum country, along the base of the mountains, until we reached a defile of the dividing ridge, called Hell's Gates, a distance from Flathead Fort of about 70 miles, general course, S.E. This place is rendered notorious as being the great war-road by which the Piegans and

Blackfeet often visit this side of the mountains; by the same pass the Flatheads and other tribes cross over to the Missouri side in quest of buffalo. The spot has, therefore, been the scene of many a bloody contest between these hostile nations.

This being the usual and only place known to the whites for passing the mountains, I hesitated for some time between two opinions—whether to cross there, or proceed in hopes of crossing somewhere else to more advantage. Difficulties presented themselves in either case : by adopting the former, we should have been exposed to the Blackfeet and other tribes during a journey of three weeks, the time we should have taken before we could reach a pass, either to get clear of those tribes, or back into the Snake country; by the latter, the road was entirely unknown to the whites, and the mountains were lofty and abrupt. Yet we decided on the latter, and determined to continue our course.

Here again the Iroquois wished to go off, saying that they would make good hunts in the recesses of these Alpine ridges; but I knew them too well to be duped by their artifices. They would have either sneaked back or lurked about among the Flatheads, and gone with them; not to hunt the beaver, nor pay their debts, for that never troubled them, but to feast on buffalo. I, therefore, got them brought round again, thinking that, if I once succeeded in getting them into the heart of the

Snake country, all would be right, and they would not be so anxious to go off by themselves.

In this encampment we remained for a day or two, and our hunters killed four wild horses. Just at the time we were starting one morning, and in the act of crossing a deep ravine not far from our camp, about twenty of those beautiful and hardy tenants of the mountain came dashing down from a neighbouring height, with their shaggy manes and long tails waving in the wind; but, with all their keen scent, the rifles of our hunters brought four of them to the ground before they had time to turn round! It is a rare thing for them to be either entrapped or approached, and our hunters were more delighted with their success in this little adventure than if they had killed a hundred buffalo. We also got twenty-seven elks and thirty-two small deer at this place, which secured the party for a while from hunger.

On leaving our encampment at Hell's Gates, I discovered that one of my Iroquois, named Jacob, had deserted. To have gone in pursuit of him would have been vain, if he wished to keep out of our way; so we continued our journey. We had not proceeded far, when the advanced party called out, "Enemies! enemies! Blackfeet!" As soon as the word "enemy" is uttered, every one looks at the priming of his gun, and primes anew; which on the present occasion was no sooner done than a party mounted on horseback advanced at full speed.

We were soon prepared to receive them, either as friends or foes. On our getting up to them, we found eight Piegans squatted down at the corner of a thicket, with their snow-shoes and other travelling necessaries at their side.

On our approach, they manifested a good deal of uneasiness: not one of them got up to shake hands with us—a custom peculiar to most Indians; but they sat still, each having his bow and arrows lying between his legs ready for action. As soon as we spoke to them, however, their fear vanished, and they became cheerful. In answer to our queries, they said, "We have come from the Missouri. There are no other Piegans in this quarter. We have been a month on our journey in search of the whites to trade." But, seeing scarcely anything with them, I asked them what they had to trade; which rather puzzled them, for they kept looking at each other for some time without giving an answer. I took them to our camp, gave them a smoke, and then warned them not to follow us, nor attempt to steal our horses; for, if they did, I would shoot them.

Trade, however, was not their object—they were scouts on the look out, from some large camp. On putting up at night, I was informed that several of the Iroquois had followed the Piegans, and traded away all their ammunition for a few useless Indian toys; one of which was a head-dress of feathers! On inquiring into the particulars, and finding the report to be true, I spoke to Pierre, the head man, and reproved them for their conduct. Elk and small deer now became abundant; so that our hunters had no difficulty in keeping the pangs of hunger at a distance. Our traps brought us twelve beaver; being our first successful attempt since we started.

The second day after passing the Piegans two of the Iroquois, named Laurent and Lizard, deserted the party, and turned back. It was some hours before I had notice of the circumstance. Now that they had begun, there will be no end to desertion thought I, if a stop is not speedily put to it: because Jacob got off clear, others will think to do so. Losing no time, I took four men with me, and hurried after the fugitives. It was a leap in the dark; for they might have hid themselves so well in a few minutes' time that we could never have found them out; but we came upon the fellows as they were making a fire at the distance of sixteen miles off, and so surprised were they that they took no steps to get out of the way. We at once laid hold of them, but could not by fair means prevail upon them to return; we, therefore, had recourse to threats, being determined, since they gave us so hard a ride, not to deal too softly with them. Lizard, in particular, would neither lead nor drive, and we threatened to drag him back at one of the horse-tails before he consented to go. Back, however, we brought them; but, having to sleep on the way, we had to keep watch over the rascals all night. On the next day we got back to the party early, raised camp, and proceeded; but we had not gone far before the cry of "Enemies! enemies!" was again raised. A party immediately pushed on a-head, when the supposed enemies turned out to be friends; they were six Nez Percés, whom we had supposed to be horse-thieves, as none of them had saddles, and yet they were driving horses before them.

Although we had no danger to apprehend from these people, yet their presence annoyed us, for it still kept a door open for some of our party to desert; so we got clear of them as soon as possible, and hastened on our journey. Before parting, however, Vallade, one of the Spokane Indians belonging to our party, wished to accompany them. Vallade was a good fellow in his way; but, not being accustomed to long journeys, he grew fainthearted; so I gave him his discharge, and he turned back.

As we left the Indians, however, four of the Iroquois kept in the rear, and exchanged with the Nez Percés two of their guns for horses! If they had not guns to defend themselves, they had a relay of horses to carry them out of danger. Such improvident and thoughtless beings as Iroquois should always be restricted to their hunting-implements; all the rest goes in traffic among the natives, to no purpose.

During some days past the weather had been

very severe; so that many of the old as well as young were severely frostbitten in their fingers, noses, cheeks, and feet. At every encampment more or less beaver were caught daily. Elk, deer, and mountain goats became very numerous; so that our new regulations made us fare well in the way of provisions. Had it been our lot to pass here in summer instead of in winter, there are many level spots and fertile valleys that, from the appearance of the country, might invite the husbandman and the plough.

After putting up one evening, the uncommon noise made by the wolves about our camp annoyed us. At last, it struck me that it might be wolves on two legs, imitating the animal; and as the place was very suspicious I doubled the night-watch, and we laid down in our clothes, but passed a restless night. In the morning, however, all was safe, and we were early on our journey. In no place of our trip, Hell's Gates itself scarcely excepted, did we meet with such a gloomy and suspicious place. At every bend of the river, wild and romantic scenes opened to view; the river alone preventing the hills and cliffs from embracing each other. We had to cross and recross twelve times in half as many miles, until we reached a rocky and slippery path on its margin, where grew a few pine-trees, through which the narrow and intricate path led.

Out of one of the pines I have just mentioned,

and about five feet from the ground, is growing up with the tree a ram's head, with the horns still attached to it; and so fixed and imbedded is it in the tree, that it must have grown up with it: almost the whole of one of the horns, and more than half of the head, is buried in the tree; but most of the other horn, and part of the head, protrudes out at least a foot. We examined both, and found the tree scarcely two feet in diameter. Here we put up at an early hour, and called the place Ram's Horn Encampment.

Our Flathead Indians related to us a rather strange story about the ram's head. Indian legend relates that one of the first Flathead Indians who passed this way attacked a mountain ram as large and stout as a common horse; that on being wounded, the fierce animal turned round upon his pursuer, who taking shelter behind the tree, the ram came against it with all his force, so that he drove his head through it; but before he could get it extracted again, the Indian killed him, and took off the body, leaving the head as a memento of the adventure. All Indians reverence the celebrated tree, which they say, by the circumstances related, conferred on them the power of mastering and killing all animals; hundreds, therefore, in passing this way sacrifice something as a tribute to the ram's head; and one of the Iroquois, not to incur the displeasure of the god of hunters, hung a bit of tobacco on the horn, to make his hunting propitious.

Late in the evening, when our hunters, who had been in advance of the camp, arrived, they had a sad story to tell. "We have been," said they, "at the head of the river; our travelling in this direction is at an end: the mountains a-head surround us in all directions, and are impassable; the snows everywhere beyond the banks of the river are from eight to ten feet deep, and that without a single opening or pass to get through; so that we may as well turn back without going further, for we shall have to go by Hell's Gates at last." Discouraging as these accounts were, we made preparations to advance; for I was determined not to turn back, while I could advance. Leaving, therefore, Ram's Horn Encampment, we proceeded in various directions, often making several traverses through ice and snow; we then left the river, and crossed what we called the Little Mountain; the ascending and descending of which occupied us many hours in putting two miles behind us. Regaining the river, we continued our journey until we reached a little fork, where two small streams crossed each other at right angles, in the middle of a deep valley, hemmed in by lofty mountains; the appearance of which seemed strongly to confirm the opinion of the hunters, that we could proceed no further in the present course. Here we made a pause, and all gazed in wonder at the bold and stupendous front before us, which in every direction seemed to bid defiance to our approach. This gloomy and discouraging spot we reached on the 12th of March, 1824, and named the place "The Valley of Troubles."

March 13th.—Our situation and the hopeless prospect before us made me pass a sleepless night; but on going through the camp this morning, I found many, and the Iroquois in particular, with a smile of gratification on their countenances, at the idea of their having to turn back: the very idea of such anticipations on their part aggravated the evil on mine. After putting the camp in a position of defence—for we had now to consider ourselves in an enemy's country—I took six men with me and proceeded in the direction our road lay, in order to reconnoitre the passes in the mountains. We set out on horseback, and finding in one place an opening, out of which issued a small rivulet, we followed it up about four miles or more, till we reached its head, the source of the Flathead River; but not finding a pass to advance further with horses, we tied them, and proceeded on foot. At the head of the rivulet or creek we ascended one of the mountains for more than a mile, till we reached the top, where it was level ground; but the snow there was seven feet deep; nor could we form any idea as to the nature of the country further on, it being thickly covered with timber. So we returned, took our horses, and got back to the camp late in the evening, to pass another comfortless night.

March 14*th.*—During this day, I got six of my most trusty men ready, with snow-shoes and four days' provisions, and sent them across the mountains to ascertain the depth of snow, the nature of the pass, and the distance to the other side. Their instructions led them to follow the road along the creek, where I had been on the 13th. We shall now leave them to pursue their journey, while we notice the occurrences about the camp.

The men I had despatched were no sooner started, than I sent off four others, to see if any other more favourable opening could be discovered in a different direction, while I and a few others proceeded in another quarter; but both parties proved unsuccessful. So we all returned, hungry, fatigued, and discouraged; and none more so than myself, although I had to assume cheerfulness, in order to encourage others.

March 15*th.*—The sun had scarcely appeared over the mountain ridges, before some of our people called out "Indians, Indians;" when we beheld, emerging from the woods, five solitary wretches on snow-shoes, coming towards our camp. On their arrival, I was rejoiced to find that they were Snakes, as I expected to get some interesting information from them respecting the mountain passes and other matters. They were, however, anything but intelligent: we could neither understand them, nor they us, consequently we could learn nothing from them.

These strangers were the very picture of wretchedness, and had a singularly-odd appearance; they were wrapped up in buffalo-hides with the hair next to their skin, and caps of wolfskin with the ears of that animal erect as if alive; and they resembled rather walking ghosts than living men. Their condition, however, excited compassion. They belonged, if we could judge from the jargon they spoke, to the mountain Snakes. Yet, with all their ignorance, I intended attaching them to our party, had not an unforeseen circumstance prevented it.

The day after the five Snakes arrived, two of the hunters came running into the camp almost breathless, calling out, "A war-party, a war-party." This announcement rather surprised me: I knew not where a war-party could come from at that season of the year, and in such a part of the country as we were in; as Indians seldom go on war expeditions during winter. We, however, got our big gun ready, match lighted, and all hands armed in a few minutes; when I observed at a short distance a large body of Indians coming down the slope of an hill, having every appearance of a war-party. On their approaching our camp, not knowing what might happen, I immediately ordered the Snakes off to the woods, telling them to join us again as soon as the storm had passed over; but we never saw them afterwards.

When the Indians who were approaching us had

got within two hundred yards of our camp, they made a halt, and collecting in a group, stood still. At this group we pointed our gun. Taking then a flag in my hand and one man with me, we went up to them; I telling my people at the time that if there was danger, or the Indians attempted anything to us, I would wave a handkerchief as a signal for them to fire off the gun at once. They, however, proved to be a mixture of Nez Percés and Shaw-ha-ap-tens, eighty-four in number, headed by two of the principal chiefs. We then all joined the camp.

Although not a war-party, nor our declared enemies, yet they are not at all times friendly when abroad, and I could have very well dispensed with their visit; but under existing difficulties, they were hailed with a heart-felt welcome by most of my people, particularly the Iroquois.

It will be recollected, that some time ago we fell in with six Nez Percés, with whom two of my Iroquois had exchanged their guns for horses; which horses, it would appear, did not belong to the fellows who had sold them, but belonged to our visitors: the chiefs claimed them as soon as they arrived, mentioning the six Nez Percés, and the place where they had stolen the horses. The Iroquois had therefore to deliver them up; and I was not displeased at it. When the Indians were going off, however, I interposed in behalf of the Iroquois, and the chiefs consented to give them two old guns in lieu of the new ones they had given for the horses.

On this occasion, the head chief told me that since we had passed Hell's Gates, the Blackfeet had stolen, at two different times, 135 of the Nez Percés and Flathead's horses. He also informed me that five of the Snakes had been at the camp of the former on an embassy of peace, succeeded in the object of their mission, and returned loaded with presents: it was not likely, however, that the five wretches we had seen were the delegates spoken of. In reference to the pass through the mountain, the absorbing question with me, the chief observed that we could not possibly pass before the month of May; and then the only practicable road was in the direction my men had gone: information which was not calculated to cheer us in our present situation. At the expiration of two days all the Indians left us, but not before they had rifled the unprincipled Iroquois of almost every article they possessed, in exchange for Indian toys.

Expecting hourly the return of the six men I had sent across the mountain on the 14th, I had been revolving in my own mind the best plan to be pursued. In the meantime, however, as I expected their report would be such as would rather discourage any further advance, and as such might have a decided effect on the conduct of my people, I resolved on going to meet them, in order to prepare their report before it reached our camp, and to place it before the people in its most encouraging features. So I set off under the pretence of going to hunt; but after proceeding some five or six miles, and waiting all day, I returned at night unsuccessful, telling my people of course that I had seen plenty of game, but failed in killing any.

I passed a sleepless night, and getting up early the next morning, and telling my people that I was going off again to hunt, I set out to wait, with anxious forebodings, the arrival of my men. I had not been long at my station before I was agreeably relieved by their arrival; and the more so by their having loads of buffalo meat on their backs: a very welcome article to us in our situation, for animals had become very scarce about the camp, and our hunters had to go a long distance before finding any. The men had been six days on their journey, and two of them were almost snow blind: this grievous and painful malady often afflicts people travelling on snow in the spring of the year. We, however, sat down on the crust of the snow, struck a fire, and made a meal on the flesh they had brought with them. During all this time, Grand Paul, the chief man, related the story of their journey; which I will give the reader in his own words.

" From the head of the creek we proceeded across the mountain in a south-easterly direction. The first three miles were thickly wooded, and the snow from six to eight feet deep, with a strong crust on the top. Afterwards, the country became more open, with occasional small prairies here and there; the snow, however, keeping the same depth, with the crust still harder and harder on the top as we advanced, for about three miles further, till we had reached fully the middle of the mountain. From thence, all along to the other side, a distance of six miles more, the snow ranged from five to six feet deep, with the crust very strong, till we got to the open plains. The distance, therefore, across, is twelve long miles—a distance and depth of snow that can never be passed with horses in its present state. Beyond the mountain is a large open plain, over which the snow is scarcely a foot deep. There we found plenty of buffalo, sixteen of which we killed; but for want of wood and other materials we could not make stages to preserve the meat, but had to abandon it to the wolves, excepting the little we have brought with us."

Here, then, was a description of the mountain pass, as related by those who had examined it; so that we knew something of the extent of the difficulties before us. According to the plan in my own mind, I instructed the men how they were to act on getting to the camp, in order that they might not discourage the people; who at this time required but the shadow of an excuse to turn back. "Pass we must," said I to them. "You will, therefore, proceed to the camp—without, however, letting any one know that you had seen me—and the story that you will tell there will be thus: that the mountain is only eight, instead of twelve miles"—for it appeared to me very possible that the men themselves might have exaggerated the distance; "that, after the first three miles, the snow gets less and less; and that a south wind, with a few fine days, which we may now hourly expect, would soon reduce the quantity of snow. The [difficulty of passing will be easily overcome; and once on the opposite side, buffalo for ourselves and grass for our horses will be abundant. Thus a few days' exertions would put all our troubles and difficulties behind us, and in plenty of beaver we should soon forget our toil, and make up for lost time."

The men went off to the camp, and did just as I had told them. I returned late in the evening, but without having killed any game; so that my people, of course, marked me down in their own minds as a blundering hunter. On reaching the camp, I of course pretended not to know of my men's arrival, went up to them, and asked the news of their trip; when Grand Paul, in the presence of all, repeated the story I had put into his mouth respecting the road, the snow, and the distance.

With all the difficulties of the undertaking pressing on my mind, I assembled the head men of the different parties, and several others; and we held a council on the steps to be taken in order to cross the mountain. But our council was very discordant. Some began by observing that the undertaking was utterly impossible; others smiled at the folly of such an attempt; while some thought it even madness to attempt making a road over such a field of snow. Nettled at their obstinacy, I instantly checked their remarks by observing that I did not call them together to decide on the possibility or impossibility of making the road, having settled that point already in my own mind; but simply to have their opinions on what they might consider the easiest and best way of doing it: for do it we must; and the sooner they became unanimous the better.

This sudden check caused such a long pause, that I got alarmed lest they would not speak at all. After some time, however, old Pierre broke silence by observing, that "We might try horses." Others remarked that "It would be sooner done on foot;" while some said nothing at all, but observed a sullen silence. The general voice, however, was for turning back. Here I had to interrupt them again. I told them turning back was out of the question. Some then observed that we might remain where we were until the fine weather would make the road for us. Old Pierre again spoke in favour of trying the road; some others spoke to the same effect. On this occasion I had every reason to be satisfied with the conduct of old Pierre, the Iroquois; while on the other hand, John Grey and his confederates opposed those who were for making the road. On this occasion the disaffected were the most listened to; and Grey opposed everything but turning back. At last, however, they all agreed to try the road any way I wished.

I then represented to them the necessity for our persevering in the direction we were in, and that without a moment's delay; that according to Paul's report, there were only eight miles, which would scarcely be 300 yards to each; and that the joint efforts of so many men and horses would soon remove the trifling difficulties before us; my opinion, therefore, was that we should set about making the road on the following day. To this they all agreed, and we parted in good spirits.

I began to think that all would go on well; but I soon found out, to my great disappointment, that what was settled within doors was soon forgotten out of doors; for when our meeting broke up, our resolutions fell to the ground. Old Pierre, even, began to waver, and for every one that was in favour of making the road, ten were against it; to add to our perplexities, there unfortunately fell, during the night, more than a foot of snow.

March 20th.—Notwithstanding the conflicting opinions regarding the road, and the unlooked-for fall of snow, I ultimately succeeded in getting forty-five men to start with eighty horses, to begin the road; and never did I set out on any undertaking with less hope of success than I did on this. On arriving at the place, we were for some time at a loss how to begin; but after a good deal of manœuvring, one man on snow-shoes took the foremost horse by the bridle, while another applied the whip, to urge the animal on. When it had made several plunges forward, it became fatigued, and would neither lead nor drive; so there we left it in the snow, with nothing to be seen but the head and ears above the surface.

The second was then whipped up alongside of the first, and urged forward, making several plunges still further on; and then it lay in the snow, some six or seven yards a-head of the other. The third did the same, and so on until the last; when nothing was to be seen of our eighty horses but a string of heads and ears above the snow! We then dragged out the first, next the second, and so on, till we had them all back again. The difficulty of getting them extricated was greater than that of urging them forward; but we were partly recompensed by the novelty of the scene, and the mirth and glee which the operation diffused among the people. All this was very well for a while; but the men, as well as the horses, soon got tired of it. This single operation, for we only went over all the horses once, occupied us nine hours; but we got 580 yards of the road half made, and returned to camp after dusk.

Our first attempt, although an arduous one, produced no very flattering result—scarcely a quarter of a mile of road; but I represented to the people that it was far beyond my expectation; though in my own mind, the task appeared beyond our means of accomplishing, and one of the most discouraging undertakings I had ever attempted. And if so hopeless under shelter of the woods, what would it be out in the open plains, where the road would be liable, from every blast of wind, drift, or snow, to be filled up in as many hours as we should spend days in opening it? I, however, put the best face on things, and did everything in my power to cherish hope, which was so necessary to encourage my people to persevere and finish the task which we had begun.

March 21st.—After some hesitation among the people, we again resumed our labours at the road; but out of forty men and eighty-five horses which had set out in the morning, twenty-eight of the former and fifty of the latter were all that reached the ground. Thus after eight hours' hard toil, in much the same way as the day before, we only made the distance of 370 yards, when dark night brought us back to our quarters. With various degrees of success, and much anxiety and labour, we continued, doing more or less each day, until the 27th, when we reached the extremity of the woods. But in the open plains our progress promised to be exceedingly slow and discouraging, both on account of the additional distance we had to travel backwards and forwards, as well as the uncertainty of the winds and drift, which filled up the road nearly as fast as we could open it. Nor had we, after eight days' harassing labour, got over more than one-third of the distance! Although, if anything, the depth of the snow had decreased, yet in no place was it under seven feet. There were also other inconveniences; the mornings were cold as in winter, but during the day the sun melted the snow on our clothes and made them uncomfortable, while in the evening they froze, and became stiff on our backs. The task was so disheartening, that on the last day I could only muster eight men and a few horses; and before night I found myself left at the task with only four of that number: I alone worked with heart and hand.

After smoking our pipes, we turned our faces towards the camp; but not to enjoy pleasure; for a dark and discouraging gloom had now spread its influence from one end of the camp to the other. Still trying, however, to show a cheerful countenance, I began to praise our exertions, and admire the progress we had made, in order to draw from the better-affected portion of my people a full disclosure of their feelings on the subject of the road; although I could read their feelings and their thoughts as well as I knew my own. Disappointment now appeared inevitable, and I had soon to regret that I had given them the opportunity of expressing themselves; for their looks alone, without words, might have convinced any man that nothing was working within but a determined stand against any more road-making. I therefore changed the subject as quickly as possible.

In this perplexing situation I felt that something must be done without delay; I therefore began to mention to them the advantages we should derive from changing our plan of proceeding altogether. Not that I really thought we could better it; but I foresaw that without something new to divert their present feelings, we should never advance.

If discouraged before, I found but little to cheer or console me in the camp. Provisions were scarce; neither did our horses more than ourselves fare too well: everything, in fact, seemed to be against us.

The greatest difficulty, however, was with the treacherous Iroquois, who in proportion as other troubles embarrassed me, never failed to take advantage of them; and at this time it was rumoured that they were trying to diffuse disaffection throughout the whole party. Perceiving a storm to be fast gathering, I prepared to avert it; and immediately convened a meeting, not only of the four principal men, as they were called—for their influence as well as their fidelity was at an end—but of all hands.

After setting forth the great progress that we had made, in so short a time, and awarding the praise that was due to their unwearied exertions, I proposed, as an improvement, that there should be a week's respite from labour, in order to lay in a stock of provisions and to give time for the snows to decrease in the mountains and on the other side; then, with a few fine days, we should be able to finish the road in a short time. And as the horse plan did not succeed well, I proposed that we should adopt a more efficient and expeditious plan of proceeding, which was this:—We should get mallets and wooden shovels made; two men, with mallets, would break the crust of the snow, the shovel men would follow them, and shovel it away, while the greater part would keep behind, packing down the snow with their feet. Twenty men would be thus employed, and the others would guard the camp, and provide food; and those who worked in the snow one day would remain in camp the next: we should thus make short work of it. Having stated my plan in a few words, I paused for their answer. Their silence was enough.

I now found, but too late, that I had committed a blunder in assembling all the camp together; for it is always easier to gain on the few than on the many. At last, they broke silence; and twenty voices spoke at once. I was mortified to find that my private instructions to Grand Paul, respecting the length of the road, had become known; which by no means mended the matter. John Grey stated, that "the road across the mountain was twenty miles, and the snows nearer twenty feet deep, than seven." Old Pierre and others observed, "We had no provisions for ourselves, and our animals were starving;" while many swore against making any more of the road: "We will neither work with mallets nor shovels." In short, the universal cry was for turning back, and relinquishing the road as impracticable. "Where are the provisions?" was the general cry; "our families are now starving." I told them that, if we had no provisions, we had hunters, we had guns and ammunition. "I will answer for provisions," said I: "let there be but a good understanding and unanimity among ourselves; secure that, and I will answer for the rest. Besides," continued I, "in accomplishing the task before us, we can boast of having done what was never before equalled by man in this country."

After some time, and a great deal of speechifying, a few of them began to relent, and expressed themselves friendly to the plan of making the road; simply, I supposed, because it was new. Among the first, were some of the Iroquois: we must give every one their due; and had I not known their character too well, I might have been led to believe that they were in right good faith. Even John Grey seemed to adopt my views; this man, an Iroquois half-breed from Montreal, and educated, had no small degree of influence over his countrymen; but he was unfortunately a refractory and base character. However, after stating my views to them, they all agreed to continue the road, after a week's respite. I began once more to entertain some hopes of success; we smoked our pipes together, and parted for the night in the most friendly manner.

Notwithstanding this apparently good understanding, I soon learnt that John Grey had been very busy in trying to poison the minds of the Iroquois and of the others, by strongly advising them to turn back and not to submit to any more road-making: he urged that I was but one man, and could not force them to it; that they had dug long enough in snow; that they would have a summer's work of it, and he doubted if they could do it in one summer; and he swore that back he was determined to go, and he would like to see the man that would prevent him. Such language, among people already tired and disaffected, had great influence.

I knew that Grey was disseminating an ill feeling in the camp, and I was of course preparing, in the isolated position in which I stood, to counteract it. Nothing, however, declared itself openly until the second day in the evening. I had hoped his machinations would have failed of their effect; but a little before sunset he came to my tent, saying that he wished to see me. I told him to come in, and, after sitting down for a few minutes, he said that "he was deputed by the Iroquois and other freemen to let me know that they regretted their promise made at the council, and could not fulfil it; that they were all resolved on abandoning the undertaking, and turning back!" He urged, "that by remaining to make the road, they would lose the spring hunt; and besides that they were tired of remaining in the large party, and wished to hunt apart: moreover, that they did not come to this country to be making roads; they came to hunt beaver. As for myself," said John, "others may do what they please, but I shall turn back: I am a free man, and I suppose I can do as I please."

John having proceeded thus far, I got out of all patience, and interrupted him, by observing "whatever you have got to say, John, on your own behalf I am ready to hear, but not one word on behalf of any one else. This," I continued, "savours very much of a combination to defraud the Company and disappoint me. You have all taken a wrong view of things: every rose," continued I, "has its thorn, John; so has the hunting of beaver. You say that by remaining to make the road you will lose the spring hunt; you will do no such thing; but by turning back you will lose not only the spring but the fall hunt. The spring here is later by a month than in any other part of the country. Your plan is a bad one; even were it at your choice, which is not the case. Follow my advice, John: I alone am answerable for your hunts. If you disliked large parties, you should have remained at home, and not have come to this country at all: small parties cannot hunt here. As to your digging in snows and making roads, it is of two evils perhaps the least: it is better for you to be making roads for a few days, than to have for many weeks to contend with a powerful and dangerous enemy; which would be the case if we passed through Hell's Gates and had to fight our way among the Blackfeet. We have all embarked on a sea of troubles; great quantities of furs are not to be secured in these parts without fatigues, cares, hardships, and perils. My advice therefore to you, and to all, is to submit to circumstances, and abandon the idea of turning back."

John, however, persisted in his opinion, and swore that neither fair words nor anything else should alter his mind, that "back he would go." "You are a most unreasonable man," replied I; "you gave your consent two nights ago; things are not worse now than they were then, and you now withdraw that consent. But I did wrong in asking your consent, I ought rather to have commanded it; and for the future I am determined to ask no man's consent: if you attempt to turn back, I shall certainly try to stop you, or any one else:" on my saying so, John abruptly got up, bade me good night, and went off.

Grey's conduct made me pass an anxious and uncomfortable night. As usual, I got up early in the morning, and soon afterwards, sure enough, as he had said, John collected, saddled, and loaded his horses ready for a start, and every eye in the camp was directed to witness his departure. Affairs had now come to a crisis; the success or failure of the expedition depended on the issue. I was determined now to act, and resolutely went up to him with a cocked pistol in my hand, ordering him either to pay his debt, or unsaddle his horses and turn them off with the others, or he was a dead man. John, seeing no person interfere, unsaddled his horses, and I returned to my tent. Not another word was spoken, and here the affair ended.

Although I had now succeeded in settling the knotty point with Grey, yet I was not altogether without my fears that something might take place to disturb our arrangements: it was evident from the sullen conduct of the Iroquois, that if left together they would still be plotting mischief. To divide them as quickly as possible was my only plan. I therefore fitted out and despatched a party of ten men to cross the mountain in pursuit of buffalo; not forgetting to place four of the Iroquois among them. The other hunters were dispersed in every direction, in quest of smaller game; and I kept my friend John Grey in the camp with myself.

The small deer had become very scarce, and in my anxiety to get a stock of provisions laid up, that we might proceed with the road, I offered a reward of a new gun to the hunter who should prove himself most deserving. This had a good effect; but as the valleys furnished but little, they had to proceed to the mountains in search of the big-horned, or mountain sheep, as they are called. A third party took to the woods to make mallets and shovels. Thus I had them all divided the next day, and this arrangement promised to preserve peace and good order for a time.

Scarcity of provisions troubled me greatly, and to ensure success as far as possible, I studied to make such a distribution of the people, that neither plots nor treachery could well be carried on without detection; and with strict economy in the camp, and an equitable division of everything that came into it, we hoped to guard against the worst. The big-horn sheep party had good luck during several days; but those animals were smaller in size than I had been in the habit of seeing elsewhere, with heads very disproportionate to the size of their bodies, and horns still more disproportionate to the size of the head. The average weight of these animals was 70 lbs., and the head of the male generally weighed as much as a third of the body, while the horns were twice the weight of the head without them. One of the ram's horns brought into our camp measured forty-nine inches in length, following the curve or greatest circle round the convex side; and the circumference in the thickest part was twenty-eight inches: this horn weighed eleven pounds.

On the seventh day after starting, the buffalo

hunters, from across the mountain, arrived successful; and our supplies from all quarters put us in possession of eight days' provisions in advance, with which we prepared to resume our labours at the road.

April 3rd.—At six o'clock in the morning, after an interval of seven days, I set out with forty men and seventy horses, with shovels and mallets for each—John Grey among the number—to resume our labours at the road. After reaching the place, however, the weather turned out so bad with sleet and snow, that we were forced to return home without doing much; and, what was still worse, many parts of the road already made were filled up again. This was a very discouraging circumstance, and caused a good deal of murmuring: indeed, the distance from our camp to the scene of operations, being not less than nine miles, and the return another nine, was of itself, without any other labour, a day's work. Many hints were given by the Iroquois that had I now and then a dram of rum to give them, my road would soon be made. I knew myself that a little, in our present state, would have done more than anything else towards hastening on the road; and I would at this time have given twenty guineas for as many pints of rum, had it been in my power to get them.

April 4th.—At an early hour this morning we were again at work, with the same number of men as yesterday. Whether from the novelty of our shovel operations, or that the new plan was better than the old one, I could not say; but we made, in the usual depth of snow and in the same number of hours, 810 yards: though we were so tired at night as to be hardly able to mount our horses.

On the 5th, with the same number of men as the day before, we only made about 450 yards, although we laboured for the same number of hours.

On the 6th we did nothing at all. I attempted to start in the morning, but the attempt proved fruitless, there being a good deal of reluctance and altercation among the parties; so that I had at last to yield to circumstances, and there was no road-making that day. I was rather apprehensive that, as the conflicting opinions were marked with a good deal of bad feeling, they would have resulted in a second break-up; but, fortunately, we got all our differences arranged, and closed the day in harmony.

April 7th.—Early this morning, I started with thirty-five men, and happening to fall on a small ridge part of the way, we succeeded in opening rather more than a mile in length, in almost bare plains. This was cheering, and greatly revived our sinking spirits; but we were kept in constant alarms, fearing the wind and drift should rise: for had it blown but an hour it might have destroyed the labour of days. Our hopes now rested on calm weather, and we had to labour day and night till we should accomplish the task before us. Six of the men volunteered to work all night, some encamped on the ground, and others went home. I was among the latter number; for I could not venture to sleep out one night, lest new troubles arising in the camp should disarrange all my plans.

April 8th.—I set out at sunrise this morning with every man and boy I could muster, leaving only five men to guard the camp; and not a murmur was heard. Our success now depending on despatch, several of the women were in attendance, with horses to carry us back at night. During last night, the six men who volunteered their services had only made about fifty yards. This day, to our annoyance, there fell a good deal of drizzling rain, which wetted us to the skin, and in the evening our clothes froze on our backs and became stiff; but the people, notwithstanding, encamped at the edge of the woods, instead of going home, so as to begin early in the morning; I and another man only returning to the camp.

April 9th.—At an early hour, and before a single man of the party who had slept out had got his eyes open, I was on the ground to rouse them up. And although we began to work somewhat later in the day than usual, yet, before night, our day's labour proved the best we had made; having with our shovels, our mallets, our feet, and the additional assistance of fifty-eight horses, beaten down a distance of nearly two miles in length. After this day's labour, and not until then, did my people entertain a hope of success: from that time we all indulged the anticipation of accomplishing our task in spite of every obstacle. The wind alone, over which we had no control, was all I now dreaded. The two next days, the 10th and the 11th, our labour was severe.

April 12th.—At five o'olock in the afternoon of this day, I with four others, after a day of severe toil, reached the other side on horseback; but being too late, and our horses too tired to return, we encamped there. The dread of the wind blowing kept me from sleeping, and when I did slumber a little after the fatigue of the day, it was only to dream of fine roads and pleasant walks, and then awake to blame my fancy for having deceived me. Nor was it till we had reached the other side, that I was fully aware of my situation; for had it come on to blow, the road through which we had forced our way would have been rendered impassible, and I should then have found myself completely separated from my people for days: all our labour and anxiety would then have been to no purpose, had my people taken advantage of the opportunity thus offered to return back. But, fortunately, the night was calm, and I got back and joined my people on the 13th.

On the 14th we raised camp, and bidding farewell to the Valley of Troubles, where we had been kept in anxious suspense for thirty-three days, we put up for the night at the head of the creek, or foot of the mountain, prior to our crossing it. And an anxious night we passed.

The spot on which we now encamped forms the extreme point of Flathead River, a distance of 345 miles from its entrance into the main Columbia a little above the Kettle Falls; of which some 250 are navigable for craft of moderate size, and the rest for loaded small canoes.

On the top of the mountain before us, over which our road led, and not more than a mile from our camp, was a small circular spring of water issuing out of the ground; I stood over it for some time, smoking my pipe, with a foot on each side of it. Yet this spring is the source, as far as I can learn, of the great Missouri River; which, after meandering through the mountain, nearly parallel with our road, crossed the grand prairie, where, uniting with several other small streams, a river fifty feet broad and about two and a half deep is formed, which then flows in an easterly direction.

April 15*th*.—Long before daylight, we were all on foot, in order to profit by the snow crust in passing the mountain. When all were ready, I took my stand on the side of the road as they began to ascend, to see that all passed. As soon as we had reached the summit of the mountain, the string, a mile and a half in length, began to form. Six men, with about thirty of the light horses, led the van; the loaded horses came next; the families followed;

and I, with four of the men, brought up the rear.

Every now and then a halt unavoidably took place. A load was upset or deranged; a horse got engulphed, or some of the families became entangled in the snow; so that it was one constant run forward and backward, lifting, adjusting, and encouraging all day. It was a novel scene in the wilderness: nothing appearing above the surface of the snow, of all that was moving, but the heads and shoulders of the riders. Children were crying with hunger, men complaining of thirst, women screaming with affright, and dogs howling; yet, amidst all this bustle, anxiety, and confusion, we pressed forward, and got safely across, after fifteen hours' exertions, just as the sun was setting, and without loss or accident to either man or beast. My hope now was, that the snow-storm might render the road behind us impassible to both man and beast; so as to prevent the Iroquois or any one else from attempting to turn back, or give us further annoyance.

But the struggle was over. The distance, however, proved to be neither eight miles, as was stated, nor yet twelve, as Paul had given us to understand, but eighteen! And, perhaps, few men in the ordinary routine of their lives in this country, ever suffered more anxiety, or laboured harder to accomplish the task they had undertaken, than we did during the past month.

Making this road through the snow took the united labour of fifty men and 240 horses, with all the other available means within our power, for twenty-one days. It must be allowed to have been an arduous undertaking, with such a medley of people and so difficult to manage; the more so, when it is taken into consideration that our supper at night depended on the good or bad luck of our hunters during the day. To their exertions and perseverance, indeed, no small merit was due.

CHAPTER XI.

Camp regulations—Beaver—Tracks of enemies—Hot spring—Snowstorm—Narrow escape—Missouri—Lewis and Clarke's track—Successful trapping — Dangerous passes — The battle — Seven trappers killed — Piegans roasted — Hardihood — Iroquois shot — Horrid cruelties — Revenge — Salmon River — Herds of buffalo — Canoe Point — Young grass—War roads — Night-watch — Heedless trappers — Martin and his horses — Scouting parties—Discouraging prospects—Hackana in favour—New prospects — Dangerous roads — Disappointments — Effect—Hackana in disgrace—A horse killed—The alarm—Escape of a child—Rock turn again—Twelve days' experience—Return to Canoe Point—The beaver cache — Swimming — Salmon River — Hot springs—Enemies appear—Pursuit—Buffalo—Forlorn trappers—Piegan war-party—Fruitless search—The mistake—Two men robbed—Looking the wrong way—Subterraneous river—A four days' ramble—Cold—Horses die—Division of the party—River Malade—Alarm—War-party—A night's dancing—Indian cunning—A horse killed—Scalps—Trapping difficulties—Watch—Perverse trappers—The alarm—Paying too dear for a drink of cold water—A horse killed—A scamper—Piegans again—Chief's declaration — New road — Frightful passes — Hard shifts — Reid's River—Dismal prospects—Disaffected people—A stand still—Two Bannatees—Their story—Three Bannatees—Their fears.

THE mountain, with all its perplexities and difficulties, being now behind us, we considered ourselves on hunting ground; and also on enemy's ground: both circumstances requiring additional care. For these reasons, new and stringent regulations, for our camp by night as well as our proceedings by day, became absolutely necessary. It was, therefore, settled, as to the night-watch, that all the horses should in future be collected every evening into one band, close by our camp, and there hobbled and guarded; and that not less than four men at a time should be on the watch after dark, to be relieved once every night, with a superintendent to each. As to our proceedings by day, it was agreed that all hands should raise camp together; that no person should run a-head, either to hunt or set traps, nor lag behind, but that while travelling they should keep close together; that no traps should be put in the water before the party encamped, and that no person should sleep out of camp. The safety and success of the expedition depending upon a rigid observance of these rules, it was decided that any individual wilfully disregarding them should be punished.

We now proposed to advance through the mountains without any plan as to our route, as the appearance of the country for beaver and other local circumstances would henceforth regulate all our movements. Leaving, therefore, our mountain encampment, we advanced in nearly an easterly direction, crossing in succession five small branches of the head waters of the Missouri. On one of these it was that M'Donald lost his man Anderson, last year, by the Piegans. After proceeding some distance, we followed down one of these creeks for upwards of twenty miles; but during all that distance we only met with one solitary tree on its banks: on this woodless creek, we encamped the second day, and took seventy beaver at the first lift. Here, however, fresh Piegan tracks were frequently seen, which admonished us to take care of our horses; the new regulations were, therefore, strictly enforced, both day and night.

At a little distance from our camp, we found one of those hot springs so often mentioned in former expeditions; but this being the first I had ever seen, I viewed it with some degree of curiosity. It was of a circular form, ten feet in diameter, but only about nine inches deep, having a white sediment at bottom; the water was reddish and tasting of iron; no grass grew about its margin. The water, although hot, did not boil.

On leaving Hot Spring Encampment the following day, and while crossing a large open plain, we were suddenly overtaken by a furious snow-storm. In a moment the day was almost turned to night, so that we got completely bewildered; one was running against another, without any knowing whither to go for shelter. In this perplexing situation I called out for each to shift for himself; and, meantime, I with some others went off, and after several hours' wandering got to some woods a little before dusk, where we passed the night. The storm continuing with unabated violence, we could not stir all the next day; the day following, however, the weather clearing up, we began to travel about in search of our lost companions, and by night we had got together once more; except two of the Iroquois and their families, in all seven persons: as their horses were found with their saddles and baggage on their backs, we expected that those unfortunates had perished in the storm. All hands were off in search of them; and we kept looking along the adjacent woods, never thinking they would have lodged in the bare plains. But I and some others happening to cross the plain where the storm had overtaken us, and seeing a dog belonging to them howling in a low place, it at once confirmed our suspicion that they had perished; we therefore approached the spot with anxious steps, and after some time we, by mere chance, found them alive: buried, however, under two or three feet of snow. As soon as the storm broke out, they had dismounted, and rolling themselves up in a leathern tent, lay quiet; they had tried to get up, and had made their way to the light of the sun, but the snow having melted upon them, their clothes had got wet, and the weather was so piercingly cold that they durst not venture to leave their hiding-place. There they had been for three nights and two days, without food or fire; and they must have soon perished for want of both, if we had not come to their relief; as they had nothing to kindle a fire, and were at least six miles from the woods. We dug them out of the snow, and wrapping them up in part of our clothing, got them to our camp; where, after some care, they all recovered.

After leaving Stormy Encampment, we wandered about through the intricate passes of the mountains, trapping and hunting with tolerable success for six days. During this time we passed the middle branch of the Missouri, and the track where Lewis and Clarke crossed over from that river to the waters of the Columbia, on their journey to the Pacific, in 1804. While in the last defile, we took ninety-five beaver in one morning, and sixty more during the same day; but the next time we set our traps, we only took three. Before we got out of part of our rugged road, we had, in one place, to ascend on the east side of a mountain for about two miles, and then descend the same on the west side. For the first mile the descent was so steep, that anything dropped from the top rolled down several hundred yards without stopping; and for the next mile in length, the intricate and tortuous windings were so short, so frequent, and so steep—sometimes up, sometimes down, side ways, cross ways, and in perpendicular steps—that we had numerous hair-breadth escapes, with ourselves as well as our horses, before we reached the bottom; which, however, we providentially did without accident.

Being now relieved from the mountains on the

east side, we considered ourselves in the Snake territory; a country comparatively more open than that which we had been wandering through for some time past. Advancing in a westerly direction, we came to that memorable spot, where, as already noticed, M'Donald had lost seven of his men in a pitched battle with the Piegans, the year before; and as we promised to notice the particulars of that unfortunate rencontre, we give it here, in the words of those who were eye-witnesses.

One day, when they had travelled until dark in search of water, they found some at the bottom of a deep and rocky ravine, down which they went and encamped. They had seen no traces of enemies during the day, and being tired, they all went to sleep, without keeping watch. In the morning, however, just at the dawn of day, they were saluted from the top of the ravine, before they got up, with a volley of balls about their ears; without, however, any being killed or wounded: one of them had the stock of his gun pierced through with a ball, and another of them his powder-horn shivered to pieces; but this was all the injury they sustained from the enemy's discharge. The alarm was instantly given, all hands in confusion sprang up and went out to see what was the matter; some with one shoe on and the other off, others naked, with a gun in one hand and their clothes in the other. When they perceived the Indians on the top of the rocks, yelling and flourishing their arms, the whites gave a loud huzza, and all hands were collected together in an instant; but the Indians instead of taking advantage of their position, wheeled about and marched off without firing another shot.

M'Donald, at the head of thirty men, set out to pursue them; but finding the ravine too steep and rocky to ascend, they were apprehensive that the sudden disappearance of the Indians was a stratagem to entrap them, when they might have been popped off by the enemy from behind stones and trees, without having an opportunity of defending themselves. Acting on this opinion, they returned, and taking a supply of powder and ball with them, they mounted their horses, to the number of forty-five, and then pursued the enemy, leaving twenty men behind to guard the camp. When our people got to the head of the ravine, the Indians were about a mile off, and all on foot, having no horses, with the exception of five for carrying their luggage; and our people, before they could get up with them, had to pass another ravine still deeper and broader than the one they were encamped in, so that before they had got down on one side of it the enemy had got up on the other side. And here again the Indians did not avail themselves of their advantage, but allowed our people to follow without firing a shot at them, as if encouraging them on; and so bold and confident were they, that many of them bent themselves down in a posture of contempt, by way of bidding them defiance.

As soon as our people had got over the second ravine, they took a sweep, wheeled about, and met the Indians in the teeth; then dismounting, the battle began, without a word being spoken on either side. As soon as the firing commenced, the Indians began their frantic gestures, and whooped and yelled with the view of intimidating; they fought like demons, one fellow all the time waving a scalp on the end of a pole: nor did they yield an inch of ground till more than twenty of them lay dead; at last, they threw down their guns, and held up their hands as a signal of peace. By this time our people had lost three men, and not thinking they had yet taken ample vengeance for their death, they made a rush on the Indians, killed the fellow who held the pole, and carried off the scalp and the five horses. The Indians then made a simultaneous dash on one side, and got into a small coppice of wood, leaving their dead on the spot where they fell. Our people supposed that they had first laid down their arms and next taken to the bush because they were short of ammunition, as many of the shots latterly were but mere puffs. Unfortunately for the Indians, the scalp taken proved to be none other than poor Anderson's, and this double proof of their guilt so enraged our people, that to the bush they followed them.

M'Donald sent to the camp for buck-shot,

and then poured volleys into the bush among them, from the distance of some twenty or thirty yards, till they had expended fifty-six pounds weight; the Indians all this time only firing a single shot now and then when the folly and imprudence of our people led them too near; but they seldom missed their mark, and here three more of the whites fell. At this part of the conflict, two of our own people, an Iroquois and a Canadian, got into a high dispute which was the bravest man; when the former challenged the latter to go with him into the bush and scalp a Piegan. The Canadian accepted the challenge; taking each other by one hand, with a scalping knife in the other, savage like, they entered the bush, and advanced until they were within four or five feet of a Piegan, when the Iroquois said, "I will scalp this one, go you and scalp another;" but just as the Iroquois was in the act of stretching out his hand to lay hold of his victim the Piegan shot him through the head, and so bespattered the Canadian with his brains that he was almost blind; the latter, however, got back again to his comrades, but deferred taking the scalp.

M'Donald and his men being fatigued with firing, thought of another and a more effectual plan of destroying the Piegans. It blew a strong gale of wind at the time, so they set fire to the bush of dry and decayed wood; it burnt with the rapidity of straw, and the devouring element laid the whole bush in ashes in a very short time. When it was first proposed, the question arose who should go and fire the bush, at the muzzle of the Piegans' guns. "The oldest man in the camp," said M'Donald; "and I'll guard him." The lot fell upon Bastony, a superannuated hunter on the wrong side of seventy; the poor and wrinkled old man took the torch in his hand and advanced, trembling every step with the fear of instant death before him; while M'Donald and some others walked at his heels with their guns cocked. The bush was fired, the party returned, and volleys of buck-shot were again poured into the bush to aid the fire in the work of destruction.

About one hundred yards from the burning bush, was another much larger bush, and while the fire was consuming the one, our people advanced and stationed themselves at the end of the other, to intercept any of the Piegans who might attempt the doubtful alternative of saving themselves by taking refuge in it. To ensure success, our people left open the passage from the one bush to the other, while they themselves stood in two rows, one upon each side, with their guns cocked; suddenly the half-roasted Piegans, after uttering a scream of despair, burst through the flames and made a last and expiring effort to gain the other bush; then our people poured in upon each side of them a fatal volley of ball and buck-shot, which almost finished what the flames had spared.

Yet, notwithstanding all these sanguinary precautions, a remnant escaped by getting into the bush. The wounded victims who fell under the last volley, the Iroquois dealt with in their own way—with the knife.

After the massacre was ended, our people collected their dead and returned to the camp at sunset; not we should suppose to rejoice, but rather to mourn. We afterwards learned that only seven out of the seventy-five which formed the party of the unfortunate Piegans, returned home to relate the mournful tale. Although our people were drawn into this unfortunate affair with justice on their side, yet they persevered in it with folly and ended it with cruelty: no wonder, then, if they afterwards paid for their cruelty with their own blood.

Leaving the scene of this tragedy, we journeyed on to the westward for some time, until we reached a strong and rapid stream about fifty yards broad, which empties itself into the Great South branch, called by our hunters Salmon River. I thought the more appropriate name would have been Lewis's Fork, as it was the first Columbia waters the exploring party fell on after crossing the Rocky Mountains. This stream forced its way through a very bleak, sterile, and rocky part of the country; yet we crossed it and ascended up the west side for upwards of ninety miles, until we got to a place called Canoe Point, where the different branches from the four points of the compass form a cross.

This stream runs in the direction of north-west. It did not prove rich in beaver, fifty-five at a lift being the most we took at one time, during our journey on it. Here in many places the snow had begun to disappear, and the young grass grew up fast; and here our horses fed, for the first time since we left Flathead Fort, without digging in the snow. The further we advanced, the scarcer were the beaver; we often took no more than twenty a day. Buffalo were abundant, immense herds of these animals being seen in every direction; but they were not fat at this season: in one of the valleys through which we passed, there could not have been less than 10,000 in one herd, out of which our hunters killed sixty; and we passed on, leaving them still feeding on the young grass. Here game of every description was in the utmost abundance, deer were feeding in herds, and wild fowls of every kind covered the waters; yet we seldom disturbed any of them, except for amusement, for our camp teemed with provisions: nevertheless, so great was the temptation, and so natural is it for hunters and trappers to waste ammunition, that all day, whether travelling or in camp, we heard shots in every direction.

With all this profusion about us, we were not exempt from anxiety; for Blackfeet and Piegan war-roads were everywhere seen, and fresh tracks of men and horses were frequent: yet it was with the utmost difficulty I could convince the people of our dangerous situation, and the necessity of watching their horses strictly at night.

One morning, on getting up at break of day (for early rising is indispensable in these parts) I found twenty-four of the Iroquois horses wandering at large among the hills; on calling the owners to account, who had been on the watch that night, I found that they had turned them out to feed: I ordered the horses to be brought in, and warned them against a repetition of such conduct. But the next morning, I found six more out of the guard, belonging to Martin, another of the Iroquois, who confessed that he had turned his out to feed; a practice neither allowed nor necessary, as our horses had always time enough to eat during the day. I immediately sent off two men for the horses, telling Martin that since he would not take care of them, I should; reminding him that he owed the Company a heavy debt, and that if his horses were stolen his hunt would be at an end, as without them he could never pay his debt, and moreover himself and family would become a burden to the camp; therefore, I should place the horses to his credit, and he and his family might henceforth provide for themselves without horses.

The next morning, on raising camp, I ordered Martin's horses to be loaded, and we set off, leaving him and his family sitting by the fire; the other Iroquois, not wishing to leave Martin behind, lent him some of their horses for the day, so that he journeyed along with us. On putting up at night, old Pierre and two others came to intercede in Martin's behalf; so, after receiving every assurance that they would all take good care of their horses in future, and observe the regulations of the camp, I delivered Martin's horses up to him: this was what I wanted; and the example had, for a long time afterwards, a good effect, not only among the Iroquois, but among the others.

In consequence of the fresh tracks of Indians which had been discovered lately, we selected a strong place for our camp; then, after delivering a fresh supply of ammunition to all hands, I sent out two scouting parties to see that there were no enemies lurking about, and at the same time to search for beaver. Both returned unsuccessful, having seen neither enemy nor beaver; one of the parties passed the defile where the veteran John Day, who died in 1819, was buried; the other party fell on a branch of Reid's River. The day following, I sent out two other exploring parties; but after two days' search, they returned, having met with very few beaver.

At last, I applied to our Snake slave for information; he gave me to understand that he knew the country well, and that there was plenty of beaver in the western quarter, but that the roads were not passable with horses. I decided on sending him and some others to visit that quarter; and at the end of three days they returned, and reported that they had not seen much, but that the further we went the more beaver we should find, and what they had seen promised well to repay the trouble of going there to trap.

I was so pleased with this information, that I gave Hackana (that was the name we had given the Snake) a second-hand gun as a present, which he was not a little proud of; and the people among themselves gave him also several trifling articles, so that our Snake guide, for we honoured him with that title, was held in considerable favour, and promised to be a useful member of our little community in future.

We had, however, reached a point where it became necessary for us to decide on the course we intended to pursue for the rest of the season. I, therefore, called all the people together, and described the country to them, and as it did not appear to me that one side was preferable to the other, I left it to them to make their choice. I then told them that the country to our left, or south-west, would lead us along the foot of the Rocky Mountains to Henry's Fork, and crossing there Lewis's River, or the main south branch, we might proceed by the Blackfeet River to the Buffalo Snakes, the Sherry-dikas, and Bears' Lake, where the country was already known; but on the other hand, if we took the west and south-west side, the country was in many places unknown to the whites, and we should have to run the risk, whether we were successful or not.

Old Pierre and some others observed, " We have already been through the country on our left, and have trapped in that quarter for two years in succession; there is nothing very inviting there; we therefore prefer trying the west quarter." This opinion they all agreed to, and it was much strengthened by Hackana's late report; so we decided on trying the unknown and unfrequented part.

Having now settled our plan of operations, we turned to the right, and entering a defile of the mountains, proceeded on the track our Snake guide had pointed out as leading to a beaver country. We advanced in the direction our guide had been, and found the rocky road most terrific; yet in the hope of soon reaching beaver, we continued till both man and horse were almost exhausted with climbing up and down; we then encamped in a place where our tired animals could not feed nor ourselves get as much level ground as we could sleep on.

Next day, we reached the point where our guide and his companions had turned back, and where it was said that the beaver would well repay the trapper for his troubles; but all we found was a small rocky creek, with scarcely any traces of that animal. We encamped, however, and, after putting one hundred and seventy traps in the water, we only got fifteen beaver. I then questioned our guide, and began to think that he knew nothing of the country, and that we had been duped. We left Creek Disappointment, and proceeded for three days further, but with no better success; here and there we found a creek of brisk running water among the rocks, but the stream seemed to be formed from the melting snow. The place having not the least signs of beaver, we encamped, and resolved on turning back by the way we came.

The people had got into a bad humour with the Snake and their disappointments in this quarter, so that they were ready to quarrel with their shadows; even the women got by the ears, and two of them fought like Amazons, until they had scarcely a rag left on their backs. From Battle River, for that was the name we gave this place, I sent off two or three parties of discovery in various directions, and taking three men with me, we proceeded on the same duty; but although we had travelled all day and slept out, such was the rugged nature of the country, that we had not made the distance of ten miles when we were stopped by perpetual snows: no beaver were to be found.

On the next morning I climbed up to the top of a high rock, but I could see nothing of the country around. This height I called Rock-turn-again; and on the top of it I deposited six balls, two flints, and a piece of tobacco; we then retraced our steps back to the camp. The other parties were likewise unsuccessful; and in their vexation, some were for stripping our Snake impostor naked, others were for tying him to a tree and leaving him.

During the day on which we arrived at this place, we had to make our way over a frightful country. In winding among the rocks on the top of one of the mountains, one of our horses was killed, and a child belonging to one of the freemen was within a hair's breadth of sharing the same fate. On this high ledge of rocks, the horses, and people leading them one after another, formed a string of nearly two miles in length; nor was there in many places room enough for a person to turn round, or look behind him, so narrow and dangerous was the pass. In this situation, a child, who had been tied to one of the saddles, happened to slide, saddle and all, under the horse's belly; when the animal took fright and began to kick, slipped over the brink of the precipice and fell down it, together with the child. The horse, getting jammed between two pieces of the rock, could not move; the mother of the child began to scream, and the alarm spread from one to another; but long before it had reached the extremity of the line, the cause of the alarm had ceased. We heard only the sound, without knowing the cause; and I and many others, thinking that we had been way-laid, and attacked by the enemy, tried to follow the sound, and reach the spot from whence it issued; but the whole party had got into confusion, and some time elapsed before we reached the place. At last, we succeeded; we then let down two men with ropes, and extricated the child; but before we had got the men hauled up again, the horse died from the injuries which it had received.

On getting back to Canoe Point, we resolved on leaving some of our beaver *en cache*, to lighten our horses; we, therefore, concealed in the face of a bank one thousand beaver, until our return. Our late trial to the west had shaken our confidence in that quarter, and many, therefore, were for abandoning it altogether; so we followed up the east branch before going again to the west.

We prepared to cross the river, and after examining it for some distance, we found a ford; but although not more than seventy-five yards broad, the current carried us so far down, that the distance between where we entered it on one side and where we got out on the other was more than two hundred yards. It being late before we got all over, we encamped for the night on the south bank.

On raising camp, we bent our course for Goddin's River, in an easterly direction; on our way thither we met with several hot springs, with which this country abounds. In one of these I was surprised to see a number of animalculæ, as large as flies, swimming about: and they seemed to thrive well in the hot element. I intended to try whether or not these little inhabitants of so warm a climate would not live in cold water, but there was not a drop to be found for miles around, and those I carried along with me died before we reached any cold water.

On passing the height of land between Salmon and Goddin's Rivers, we perceived five men on horseback coming towards us; but they wheeled about immediately on seeing us. Taking them for the advanced guard of a Piegan war-party, the alarm was given, and it being near camping time, we retreated for a short distance; then, after fixing the camp in a secure place near some woods, thirty of us mounted our horses, and set off at full speed in the direction we had seen the horsemen, in order to try and satisfy ourselves who they might be; but they having taken to the mountain we lost all trace of them. We hastened back to our camp, and after putting it in a state of defence, and setting a double guard on our horses, we passed the night in quietness, and awaited the morning in suspense; long before day, however, we were all armed and ready for what might happen; but all appearing quiet, we took a turn round before raising camp, and seeing nothing, we proceeded on our journey.

We saw but very few animals in these parts, and began to get short of provisions; for notwithstanding the abundance which we had met with on Salmon River, we had laid in but a very scanty supply, it being the custom to let the morrow provide for itself.

On reaching Goddin's River, so named after one of my men who discovered it, I sent off eight men to trap it downwards; but made them leave their horses with us, so that they might the better conceal themselves from the enemy. I promised at the same time to pick them up at the south end on a certain day, while the main party proceeded round a range of mountains in order to lay in a supply of buffalo meat; for we expected but few of these animals in the direction we were about to take: moreover, I wished to prepare some of their hides for making canoes, in case we might afterwards require them.

The second day we got to the buffalo, and encamped in Day's Valley, the spot which M'Kenzie and party visited in 1820. It was a most dreary-looking place, and the young grass had scarcely sprung out of the earth, so that our horses fared but poorly: nothing was to be seen but the tracks of buffalo and the traces of war-parties.

While our party were employed in trapping and laying in a stock of provisions, I set off with ten men to examine the country to the south-east. We were absent for four days on our trip, and at the extent of our journey we ascended a high mountain, had a good view of the country, and saw the three pilot knobs quite plain, in the direction of the east. We then passed for some distance along the waters of the main south branch, and came to a spot among the rocks which some Snakes had left in a hurry, their fire being still alive. In their little bulrush hut we found six beaver skins and several other articles, which they had abandoned through fear on our approach. We searched about and tried to find them, as I was very anxious to fall in with some of the nation, in order to obtain information about the country; but in vain. Taking the beaver away with us, and leaving instead articles of more value to them, we returned to our camp, having seen but few beaver on our trip; but the buffalo were in thousands,—a sure sign that there were no enemies about.

As soon as I reached the camp, I despatched two men to River Goddin, in order to bring back the eight men whom I had sent there to trap some time before; as we had changed our plan of proceeding, and resolved, instead of going further to the east, to turn immediately to the west, and follow up our first intention of hunting in that quarter for the season.

The two men set out early in the day, and reached the place appointed at sunset. A little before their arrival, they perceived a smoke, and taking it for granted that it must be our people, they heedlessly advanced among the bushes until they had got within gun-shot of the place, with the view of coming upon them by surprise, and frightening them; but on crossing the end of Goddin's River, which was there only a creek, when close to where the smoke arose, they suddenly perceived that they had fallen, not on their comrades, as they expected, but on a Piegan war-party. On discovering their mistake, they threw themselves from their horses, ran in among the bushes, and got into the creek; the Indians in the meantime uttering a hideous yell, seized their horses, while some others whooped and yelled about the bush in search of them. All this time they were making their way by crawling among the mud and mire under the banks of the creek, and the bushes being thick and night coming on, they fortunately got off safely, owing solely to the approach of night; their horses, their traps and their blankets, however, were carried off by the Indians. The two men continuing their flight all night and all the next day, reached our camp in the middle of the second night, in a sad plight, without shoes on their feet, and their clothes torn to rags.

After hearing their story, no doubt remained on our minds as to the fate of the eight men; so I immediately roused the camp, and we were ready for a start by break of day. Leaving fifteen men to guard and conduct the camp after us, we, to the number of thirty-five, went in pursuit of the Piegans. On arriving at the place we found the nest, but the birds had flown; so we gave up the pursuit, and proceeded up Goddin's River, in search of our eight men. We had not proceeded far, before we had the good fortune to find our men safe. They were wholly ignorant of our anxiety and their narrow escape, for they had neither heard nor seen anything of the Piegans before we reached them. It appeared that while our men were creeping through the friendly creek, which so fortunately aided their escape, they passed, unseen, within ten yards of the very men whom they had been in search of; and who were at the time, unconscious of their dangerous situation, sleeping within half a mile of the Piegan camp.

We returned to meet the main party, and reached the camp long before dark. On this disagreeable trip I lost my spy-glass. The following day, I went and examined the Trois Têtons, so named from their appearance. These three little hills, standing in a group, are very conspicuous in the middle of an open plain, having hot springs at their base; but there is no cold water nearer than the south end of Goddin's River.

On starting the next day, we proposed following up Goddin's River all the way to its source, as it had never been either trapped or examined so far before. Following up this intention, we entered it at the extreme south point, where the two men fell on the Piegan war-party. Here that river enters the ground, and wholly disappears; and the reader will be better able to judge of the body of water that is thus absorbed, when we reach its source. Following up the river for about thirty miles to the head of the main stream, we found it thirty-five paces broad, the current strong, and running over a rocky bottom. At this place, the river is formed by three branches emptying into it, one from the north-west, another from the south-east, and a third from the south, all of nearly equal size, and descending from the surrounding heights. None of them were stocked with beaver, as we only got seven from eighty traps in one night, and few nights were better: in one of the traps we caught a deer, and I mention the circumstance on account of its novelty.

We ascended the south branch, which takes its rise in a ridge of mountains that divides river Goddin on the east from Salmon River on the west, and on the very top of which we encamped on the 16th of June. From this height I despatched two parties of discovery in different directions, one of which brought us accounts of having discovered a river with considerable appearances of beaver in it, on the south-west.

The weather until that day, during the month, was extremely cold; I should suppose not less than 15° below zero on Fahrenheit's thermometer: weather for blankets, mittens, and leather coats. The ice continued thick on the water; and since the 6th instant, we had almost a succession of stormy and boisterous weather; while on the 14th there fell nearly a foot of snow: here three of our horses died from cold and fatigue.

During our journey, the Iroquois had been plotting to abandon the main party and hunt apart by themselves; more especially since my quarrel with John Grey in the Valley of Troubles, and with Martin for disregarding the regulations of the camp, and neglecting his horses on Salmon River. At last, Old Pierre was drawn into the cabal, and came to me saying, that if I would but consent to their going off, they would do much better apart. I listened with patience to the old man's representation, but did not approve of it; I then refreshed his memory with Oskononton's tale of 1819, and put him in mind of their conduct at the river Skam-naugh, and their behaviour generally when left to themselves. He still persisted, saying that they would do well, and pledged himself for their conduct. I weighed the matter in my own mind, and at last consented, thinking it better to let them go and to supply their wants cheerfully, than to be dragging a disaffected party along with us; so I fitted them out, and we parted friends: but, to my surprise, Grey and Martin gave up the idea, saying they would still prefer remaining with the main party and running all chances. When we turned our backs on each other, Pierre and his party made for the south branch; while we steered our course south-west, to the place where the discovering party had met with beaver. On Pierre's departure we arranged matters so as to meet, on the first of October, at the Trois Tétons, near Goddin's River.

On descending from the height of land, we had

to wind our steps over a prodigious elevation, the path leading along the edge of a precipice which overhung a foaming stream below; our way was full of rocks, and the place dangerous, and we had to make leather muffles for our horses' feet, as their hoofs were worn to the quick. On descending into the low bottom, we found the climate changed for the better; the snow was off the ground, the weather warm, and the new grass abundant.

Late in the evening we reached a stream, running through a deep valley, in the direction of south-west, called Rivière aux Malades; on its east bank we encamped, at a late hour.

In the vicinity of our present encampment were the finest appearances of beaver we had yet seen: in one place we counted 148 poplar trees cut down by that animal, in a space less than one hundred yards square. Our first lift was favourable, there being fifty-two beaver; in some of the traps there were eight feet, and in others seven toes, besides fifteen traps that missed altogether by the sudden rising and falling of the water: these mischances caused a total loss of thirty beaver in one night. It is always difficult and doubtful trapping where the water continues ebbing and flowing, and the chances of success are small; nevertheless, the place was promising, the weather fine, and grass good, so that our worn-out horses both fed and rested.

In the afternoon of the same day, we had to

turn our attention to something else than catching beaver, for we perceived that a Piegan war-party were descending the mountain; the cry "Enemies, enemies," sounded in our ears, and the appearance and numbers of the party justified our apprehensions, we having only three men in camp at the time.

Our first care, on perceiving the enemy, was directed to the security of our horses, which were all scattered; for this purpose, one man with some of the women and boys set off to collect and bring them into camp; but the confusion and fear operated so powerfully on them, that they made but little progress—some drove them one way, some another, so that considerable time elapsed before they were got into a narrow point behind the camp.

While the people were securing the horses, the other man and myself lost no time in getting our gun pointed, the match lit, and the women and children out of the way. Whilst all this was going on, the uproar in the camp was great, and being placed along the woods, it presented an appearance of large numbers, which made the enemy still more doubtful of attacking us.

As soon as the Indians appeared on the heights, and long before we saw them, they were discovered by some of our hunters; who, communicating their fears to each other, scampered off in every direction to avoid the enemy and reach the camp; some throwing their beaver away, others their traps, while a few abandoned their horses, traps, beaver, and all, and took to their heels, hiding among the rocks. The Indians observing these movements, took us to be more numerous than we were, and this was no doubt the chief cause why they did not at once make a rush on our horses and carry them off: which they might easily have done.

The Indians had no sooner descended into the valley, where we were busied running after our horses, than they assembled in a group together, as if counselling for a moment; then extending themselves they made a demonstration of attack. The only reason we could assign for their not carrying it into effect, was their seeing so many of our people here and there on horseback making for the camp; or perhaps they had no ammunition, for they well knew that the whites were seldom short of that necessary article, and would have given them a warm reception. A party of them intercepted two of our men, John Grey and another Iroquois, and wrested a rifle from the hands of the latter, but they instantly restored it again, on perceiving some of our people in an opposite direction.

At last, the whole cavalcade advanced towards our camp in slow procession; but our people who had made for the woods coming fast in by ones and twos, soon relieved my anxiety, for by the time the Indians had got within a hundred yards of the camp, there were thirty men in it. I went out with a flag to meet the Indians, and motioned to them by signs not to approach the camp, but to sit down and smoke where they were; they did so, and in the meantime, giving them some tobacco and leaving Kouttanais Jacques to smoke with them, I returned to the camp, where we were ready to receive them.

When all our people arrived, and I found that the Indians were only ninety-two in number, I invited them to our camp, where they passed the night in smoking, dancing, and singing. All our people were under arms; at the same time, and as a further security, I ordered forty of their horses to be hobbled and put in with ours. I also secured their guns. On the following morning I invited them together, and questioned them as to their business in that quarter; asking them if there was not land enough in their own country for burying-ground, without coming to the Snake country to trouble the whites and frighten the natives.

The chief replied, "We have been on an embassy of peace to the Sho-sho-nes. When we left our own country, about three months ago, our party consisted of three hundred men; but not finding the principal Snake chiefs, we went off to try and fall in with our friends the Flatheads; and the main party returned home." On questioning them about the party who had seized the horses belonging to the two men at Goddin's River, they denied all knowledge of that affair. I then said, "You tried to rob one of my men of his gun yesterday?" For this the chief apologized, saying, "that they only wanted to look at it, as it was a custom among Piegans to handle and look at every strange gun they might see." But their excuse carried an air of falsehood on the face of it.

I strongly suspected that they were the very same party which had taken the two horses; and, moreover, that they were not a party on an embassy of peace to the Snakes, as the chief had stated, but a scouting expedition, on the look-out to take vengeance on the whites for the misfortunes that had happened to their people in the affray between them and M'Donald's party last year: but the severe handling they had met with on that occasion, made the present party hesitate to attack so formidable a body of whites as we were; particularly since they had failed to surprise us.

Being harassed by the frequent appearance of such visitors, and this party being completely in our power, I intended giving them a fright, in return for many they had given us; I therefore seized on two of their horses and four of their guns, and told them I had done so, as a remuneration for the loss of our two horses and traps at Goddin's River—for I suspected them of taking them: "and besides," I said, "you give us too much trouble, and prevent us from hunting and trapping quietly in a country that you only frequent for mischief." This declaration humbled them: they made a thousand protestations of innocence; adding, that they were always friends to the whites; and although I did not believe a word they said, yet as there was a possibility of their being innocent, I restored the guns and horses, telling them to take care for the future.

After smoking and talking, I gave the chief five balls, powder, and a piece of tobacco; when, according to Indian custom, they exchanged some horses with our people, in token of friendship.

It was, however, amusing to witness their manœuvring in going off; some went one way, some another, dispersing here and there in small parties until they had got to a considerable distance from our camp; then assembling in a crowd, they stood for some minutes, and marching off in a body, took to the mountains. For a little time we could not account for the manner of their departure, till some one observed that none of them had gone off in the direction that the big gun was pointed.

As soon as they were out of sight, taking some men with me we mounted our horses, and went to a neighbouring height a few miles off, to watch their motions; and there we saw them join the main party, which the chief had told us had gone home. As soon as they had joined together, they sat down, as we supposed to recount their adventures; after which, they all marched off, taking the direction of the Missouri.

On the next morning, the neighbourhood being

clear of enemies, different parties were sent off in search of the traps and beaver that had been thrown away on the first appearance of the Piegans; all of which we had the good fortune to recover. At the place where the Indians had made their demonstration of attack, our people found six scalps stretched on circular bits of wood, and not yet dry!

The day after this bustle we took sixty beaver; but taking only eight at the next trial, we moved our camp down the river, and passed a bad night, from a storm of thunder and lightning.

From this place we advanced by slow marches, for five or six days, further down, till we reached a branch of the river coming in from the west, which we named West Fork; and although the appearances of beaver were favourable, yet our successes came far short of our expectation, owing chiefly to the unsettled state of the water. One morning, we found in our traps no less than forty-two feet and toes of beaver that had thus escaped!

As the generality of our readers may not be acquainted with the process of trapping beaver, we shall here explain the causes of our failure. From the great heat during the day, the snow melted so fast that the water rushed down the mountains, causing a sudden rise in the river; but the cold nights as suddenly checking that rise, its fall became as rapid; hence the cause of our traps missing so frequently. When a trap is set for the purpose of catching beaver, it requires about six inches of water over it, and still deeper water near it; because the moment the animal is caught, which is invariably by the foot or toes, it plunges and drowns. But should the water rise for several inches higher, the animal can then swim over the trap without its feet touching it, and of course gets clear. On the contrary, should the water fall several inches lower, so that the animal, on being caught, could not, from the shallowness of the water, plunge and drown, it cuts its foot or toes off, and makes its escape; thus, in either case, a loss ensues. Our success had, however, during several nights past, averaged fifty-five beaver at a lift.

Here we found black and red currants ripe: we also saw the swallow, the blackbird, and wild pigeon for the first time this season. During the mornings and evenings the mosquitoes were very troublesome.

When we first fell on Rivière aux Malades, I had intended trapping it from end to end before leaving it; but being anxious to reach Reid's River early, and finding West Fork leading in that direction, I changed my first plan. Leaving, therefore, the river, to be taken on our way back in the autumn, we resolved at once on proceeding up West Fork. Having finished trapping at its entrance, we made preparations for advancing to Reid's River, in the hope of reaching it as high up as possible, in order to trap it downwards.

For this purpose I directed the main party, on

raising camp one morning, to proceed in that direction; while I and four men with me were to remain until the return of part of our people who had gone out in search of their traps, when we were to have brought up the rear, and followed after. Turning, therefore, their backs on Rivière aux Malades, the main party continued their journey, whilst I and the men with me remained at the place appointed; which was the top of a high hill, not three miles from the encampment we had just left. From this height, however, the weather being very sultry, we descended a winding pass to the creek below, in order to refresh ourselves with a drink of cold water.

During our stay the men we had been waiting for had passed us unnoticed; but they had not got far before they met a courier from the main party a-head with the news that the Piegans were at the camp. Two of the men, therefore, wheeled round, and came back to look for us; but we had passed unseen, and they only discovered us on their return. On seeing them coming as it were from the camp we had left that morning, we very naturally supposed them to be the men we had been waiting for; but were a little uneasy at the gestures they were making to hurry our departure, and still more so on hearing them vociferously call out, "Enemies! Enemies at the camp!" and seeing them start off in the direction of the main party.

To extricate ourselves from our dangerous

position and ascend the hill again was a work of some time: we, however, made all haste; the more especially as we took it for granted that the enemy spoken of were at the camp behind us Ascending, therefore, to the top of the hill, in order to pursue our journey, and then seeing none of our people, we drove off at full speed, every now and then looking behind us. We had the distance of ten miles to go before we could join our companions, or get any support; three of our horses got completely knocked up, and falling down with the excessive heat under their loads, we, almost exhausted from fatigue, left them to their fate.

At last we came up with the party, and found to our surprise that, instead of running from the enemy, we had been running to meet them; for there they were before us. The Piegans all the time continued standing in a body, not far from our people, as if determined to oppose our progress further; or perhaps, rather hesitating whether to advance or retreat. Provoked by the loss of our horses and the continual annoyance of the enemy, I immediately served out ammunition to our people, and then told them we should go and put an end to this state of anxiety; so, leaving only the big gun and five men to guard the camp, forty-five of us mounted our horses and set off, with the full determination of having a brush with the Piegans. When we were within one hundred yards of the party, who were all on foot, two of them, with a kind of flag, advanced to meet us; we made signs for them to keep off; they, however, continued advancing. We then presented our guns at them, though I gave strict orders not to fire; but they still unflinchingly advanced: so we resolved to wait their arrival, and see what they had got to say.

The principal man, on reaching us, presented me with his flag; then, clasping my horse's neck in his arms, he began to crouch in a supplicating manner. I gave him a push off with the butt-end of my gun, which I was immediately sorry for; he nevertheless still held fast hold of my horse by the neck. We then dismounted, and entered into a parley with them. They proved to be Piegans, and 110 strong, but badly armed; having only twenty-three guns, and scarcely a load of ammunition; but they had quivers well filled with arrows.

Seeing there was no appearance of coming to blows, I invited the two Indians to our camp, intimating to them that the others should remain where they were. On reaching the camp, I despatched some men for the horses that we had abandoned on the road; two of which, together with the property, were recovered, but the third had died.

I then questioned the Indians, as we had done the party before, as to their business in that quarter; for we had flattered ourselves that we should have been, at all events, clear of both Piegans and Blackfeet in that direction. On putting the question, the chief smiling said, "We are not horse-thieves; for if we had been so inclined, we might have easily taken yours, as we were among them two nights ago. Two of my people entered your camp at night; and as a proof of what I say, one of them took a piece of deer's meat which was roasting at a fire, and stuck it on a pole at one end of your camp, and rubbed two spots of red paint on a riding-saddle at one of the tent-doors. We are, therefore, not looking for horses, nor wishing to injure the whites; but have come in search of sixteen of our relations, who came to this quarter last year, and have not been heard of since: that is our business at present."

The circumstances mentioned by the chief, respecting the roasted venison and riding-saddle, were correct. We had noticed both, but never thought that they had been the work of Indians; and it was certainly a broad hint for us to guard the camp better another time. We then questioned the chief as to the affair at Goddin's River, and gave him an account of the party we had seen at our first encampment on Rivière aux Malades; but he denied all knowledge of either.

For the fellow's candour and honesty I gave him ten balls and powder, a piece of tobacco and a knife, and shaking hands with them, we parted good friends.

From Piegan Encampment, a name we bestowed on this place, we continued our journey onwards from the head of West Fork, over a rugged country, in search of Reid's River; and although scarcely thirty miles distant, it took us six long summer days to accomplish it. During one of those days, we travelled ten hours before we made three miles : never did man or beast pass through a country more forbidding or hazardous.

The rugged and rocky paths had worn our horses' hoofs to the quick, and we not unfrequently stood undecided and hopeless of success. However, after immense labour, toil, and hardship, we reached the river. Arriving on its rocky banks, and looking, as it were, over a mighty precipice, into the gulf below, we were struck with admiration at the roaring cataract forcing its way between chasms and huge rocks over a bed it had been deepening for centuries. But although we had reached the river, we had still little hope of making our way along its precipitous bank : we journeyed on, however, sometimes in sight of it, and at other times miles from it, until we had made the distance of 116 miles; which took us twelve days, during which time we only caught fifty-one beaver.

But bad roads were not the only obstacles we had to overcome : we had starvation to contend with; for animals of the chase, of every kind, as well as beaver, were scarce, and our hunters often returned to camp more hungry and dissatisfied than they left it. At this stage of our journey the people began to murmur greatly against the roads and want of provisions—evils we could neither foresee nor prevent.

I now found that, although I had got rid of most of the Iroquois, I had not got rid of troubles; for there remained John Grey and Martin, who were enough to poison the minds of the rest. I, therefore, assembled all hands together, and told them that we had met with nothing but what we might have expected; that as we had proceeded so far in that direction, I was determined to proceed further and make the best of it, to see its good as well as its bad side; that in the nature of things we must soon get to a better part of the country than this in which we had been involved for some time past; that a few days' perseverance might bring us relief, as we should soon get to the Snakes in the direction we were pursuing; but that if a week did not procure us the relief they desired, I would be prepared to meet their views. They all consented, and order was again restored; but had they had plenty of ammunition at the time, they would have followed their own inclinations.

We had for some time past been anxiously looking for some of the Snakes, from whom we might get information respecting the roads and country through which we had to pass; we had come to some places where they had been encamped, but they always got the start of us, and having fled to the rocks, eluded our search. But as we were pondering over our difficulties, two wretched beings were found among the rocks. They proved to be the sole remnant of a small band of the Bannatee tribe, consisting of eighteen persons, whom, according to their own account, the Piegan party we had seen at West Fork had fallen upon, killing every man, woman, and child, excepting only the two men before us. These poor creatures were almost unintelligible through fear; we nevertheless comprehended their misfortunes. They were mourning, had cut their hair, and were apparently destitute of food and raiment. We could scarcely get any information from them, but understood the roads were impassable. We gave them a few trifles, and let them go back to their strongholds again.

Not an hour after the two Bannatees had gone off, a party whom I had sent out on discovery arrived at the camp with two men and a woman, whom they had surprised and brought by force; but the captives were so frightened that neither kindness nor presents could make them speak, or look upon us as friends. So we had to let them go as they came; and we remained just as ignorant as we were before, as to the roads and country.

CHAPTER XII.

A calm after a storm—Gloomy aspect—Cheering prospects—Plenty, and smiling countenances—Pee-eye-em and suite—His manner—Cayouse plenipotentiaries—The peace—A ride round the great Snake camp—The council—Ceremony of smoking—More honour than comfort—A supperless night—Peace concluded—Escort—Barter with the Snakes—The three rivers described—Beaver—Division of the party—Horse-racing—An Iroquois outwitted—The trick—Indians at home—Awkward position of the whites—Ama-ketsa—The crafty chief—Encamp in a wrong place—Excursion round the camp—Salmon—War-are-reekas—Their character—The trap quarrel—Conduct of the whites—Seize ten of the Snake horses—Rogues surprised—Stratagem—A camp cleared—The pipe stem—Stolen traps restored—Return of good feelings—Raise camp—Waterfalls—Salmon-fishery—News of the Iroquois—Point Turnagain—Comparison of distances—Natural bridge—Subterraneous river—Hot and cold springs—Valley of lightning—Thunder—Rivière aux Malades—Poisonous beaver—A horse drowned—Snake surprised—Bannatees in winter—Hazardous travelling—Mount Simpson—The Governor's punch-bowl—Source of Salmon River—Conjectures—The wounded pheasant—Bear River—A bear hunt—The bear and the beaver—The last shift—A horse drowned—Hard work and little progress—Canoe Point again—Disabled horses—Narrow escape—A man died—Buffalo plenty—The wounded bull—Habits of the buffalo—Iroquois arrive—Their story—Their conduct—American trappers.

NOTWITHSTANDING that we had seen some of the Snakes, as we so much desired, we still remained as ignorant of the country as ever. Following up the plan we were pursuing, we left the encampment, and proceeded down Reid's River. At the end of three days' toil we got clear out of the mountains, and into a highly picturesque and open country, well furnished with animals of the chace. Our first lift of beaver was sixty-four, a number considered favourable in comparison with what we had been doing for some time past. Added to this cheering prospect, six elks and seventeen small deer coming into camp at once, filled a starving and dissatisfied people with abundance. And now, for the first time during the last twenty-five days, I witnessed a smile of content throughout the camp.

The lower part of Reid's River furnishing us with plenty of beaver and other animals, raised once more a hope of making good hunts; and, for a time, my people were cheerful, industrious, and obedient. Here we had a visit from Pee-eye-em, one of the principal personages of the country, accompanied by a retinue of forty warriors, all armed with guns and mounted on horseback. They had a flag, the one given them by M'Kenzie, and arrived in state. This chief was the great sachem, so frequently and favourably mentioned by our friends on former expeditions; always remarkable for size, he had certainly not diminished in his proportions; he was dull and heavy in his manner, never smiled, and spoke slowly, in a low tone of voice. His answers were generally a nod of the head; leaving us often to guess whether he meant an affirmative or a negative. Both himself and his escort were as fine a set of athletic men as I had ever seen in the country.

Pee-eye-em appeared pleased to see the whites again on his lands, and often inquired with great eagerness about Mr. M'Kenzie. I offered the chief some tobacco; but, preferring his own, he declined taking ours. After remaining for some time with us, he told me that his camp, or the Sherry-dikas, was far off, and that he had come a journey of ten days to visit his friend Ama-ketsa, the principal War-are-reeka chief; whose camp, he said, was only a few miles distant: this was the great Snake camp mentioned to us by the Piegan chief while at West Fork. Pee-eye-em then informed me that while he was at Ama-ketsa's camp, a party of the Cayouse tribe from Fort Nez Percés had arrived there on a mission of peace; and that, hearing o the whites being in the neighbourhood, he had come to invite me to their council, in order to see the peace ratified.

Putting my people in a secure place, and taking ten men with me, and also the Indian flag, I accompanied Pee-eye-em and his followers to the War-are-reeka camp; where we all arrived at dusk, after a hard ride of ten miles. Here I met my Cayouse friends, who were no less rejoiced to see me than I was to see them in a strange country.

On the whole, nothing could possibly have happened better, than that the person who had been at the beginning of the peace, and instrumental in bringing it about, should have arrived so seasonably to witness its conclusion. The business was introduced at once. Each spoke in his turn, and I among the rest. When we had concluded, Pee-eye-em mounted his horse, with a singularly-painted robe thrown round him, and rode about for some time haranguing the people; and every now and then, the cry Ho! ho!! ho!!! was uttered by the surrounding multitude by way of confirmation. Then a number of the elderly men, collecting in a group, held consultation; when they all uttered in a loud voice and drawling tone the same cry, which appeared to convey the general consent: it only wanted the ceremony of a council and smoking to conclude the business.

The chief's lodge was quickly put in order, with a fire in the centre, when the ceremony of ratifying the peace, according to Indian form, commenced. The two Cayouse plenipotentiaries were placed in the back part of the tent by Pee-eye-em, and I next to them; eighteen Snake dignitaries next entered and squatted themselves down on each side of us. Lastly, Pee-eye-em sat opposite to us, with his back to the door, having Ama-ketsa on his right and another chief on his left; apparently with the intention of keeping out all intruders, and preventing any one from either going out or coming in during the solemn sitting. This completed the diplomatic circle. After which a silence ensued for some time.

The great medicine bag was then opened and the decorated pipe of peace taken out of it; the pipe was then filled, with the usual formality, by Pee-eye-em, who immediately afterwards took a handful or two of sand with which he covered a small hole by the fireside; then smoothing it over, he made two small holes with his finger in the sand, large enough to hold a goose's egg, one on each side. This done, he then took out of the medicine bag a small piece of wood shaped like a sugar tongs, with which he took up a piece of burning horse-dung and laid it in the hole of sand to his left; resting the bowl of his pipe in the hole to the right, and holding the stem of his pipe all the time in his left hand. He then took up the same piece of wood or tongs, and with it took the burning piece of horse-dung out of the hole to the left and laid it upon his pipe; which was no sooner lighted, than Pee-eye-em taking up the pipe with both hands, drew three whiffs, allowing none of the smoke to escape, but swallowing the whole of it; then taking the pipe from his mouth, he held it vertically each time that he smoked, blowing the cloud out of his mouth on to the stem: this he did three successive times, and each time he uttered a short prayer, as if invoking a blessing.

Then holding the pipe horizontally, and pointing

to the east, he drew three whiffs, blowing the smoke on to the stem as before; then turning it to the west, next to the south, and lastly to the north, he did the same: always observing to repeat the short prayer, when he turned the pipe. Lastly, pointing the pipe to the ground, he drew three whiffs, blowing the smoke, as before, on to the stem; signifying that the animosities of war might be for ever after buried beneath the earth. But in all this ceremony, Pee-eye-em did not once, as is generally customary among Indians, hold the pipe to, or blow the smoke, either to the sun or the firmament.

All this time Pee-eye-em was sitting on his hams; but now rising up, and turning the pipe stem, he presented it to one of the Cayouses, telling him to touch it with his mouth but not to exhale any smoke; the Cayouse did so: then withdrawing the pipe for a moment, he presented it to him a second time, with the same positive injunction, which the Cayouse observed. The caution was no doubt intended to impress upon the Cayouse the duty of reflecting on the responsibility of what he was going to do; for smoking with Indians on such occasions is the same as an oath with us: then putting it to his mouth the third time, the chief said, "You may smoke now;" adding, after he had drawn a few whiffs, "we are now brothers."

The Cayouse after smoking, handed me the pipe, but without any ceremony. The smoking then went round and round the circle, with no other formality than that Pee-eye-em always filled the pipe and lighted it himself, with the same tongs as before. The fire was always a piece of horse-dung, till the ceremony on the part of Pee-eye-em was gone through.

The lodge during this time was like an oven, so that I got up to go out and get a little fresh air; but Pee-eye-em shook his head, and made signs for me to sit down again. I then asked for a drink of water; but Pee-eye-em giving another shake of the head, I had to sit down and compose myself: there we sat, half roasted, half stifled, thirsty, and uncomfortable, until long after midnight; when Pee-eye-em getting up and opening the door went out; we all followed, and the ceremony ended.

I expected that the chief would have invited me and the Cayouses to supper and to pass the night in his tent; but supperless and houseless we had to pass the night in the open air, in a camp stinking with rotten fish, and pestered with snarling dogs: the night being warm, the stench was horrible. Next morning, seeing no signs of anything to eat, I purchased two fine fresh salmon, which my men cooked, and on which we made a hearty breakfast. We then prepared to return to our camp, and I invited the Cayouse chiefs to accompany us; but just as we were mounting our horses, Pee-eye-em, with his flag in his hand, and a retinue of forty followers, joined and accompanied us back to our camp. Comparing things, I thought that there was more honour than comfort in the Snake camp.

From the solemnity observed, it might have been expected that we were all in earnest; but so changeable and treacherous are savages, that I was apprehensive the Cayouse envoys would not get back safely; I therefore invited them to our camp, promising them an escort to convey them out of danger: we learned afterwards that they returned to their own people in safety.

The peace having been occasionally progressing for the last seven years, I now, for the first time, began to entertain hopes that it might, after all, be lasting. The hostile feelings had of late much diminished, otherwise the Cayouses would never have ventured so far, and in such small numbers, into the heart of their enemy's country. The Snakes had also, as we have already noticed, been at the Nez Percés camp, and returned with a favourable impression.

We have noticed that Pee-eye-em accompanied us to our camp, where, having remained for the greater part of two days, he returned home; on which occasion, I presented him with a hundred balls, and powder, and some few trifles, for which he appeared very thankful. We parted with regret; for the more I knew of him the better I liked him. He was sincere, well-disposed, and much attached to the whites. From this time forward, the Snakes became constant visitors at our camp;

but were not always so friendly as I could have wished. We, however, occasionally bought a few salmon from them, so that they might become possessed of some useful and necessary articles; but especially to keep up a good understanding with them. A needle was given for a salmon, an awl for ten, and a knife for fifty! and they could have enriched themselves at that rate, had we been able to encourage the trade.

After our Snake visitors had left us, we continued our trapping down Reid's River with good success, taking from seventy to eighty beaver every morning until we reached its mouth; a distance from where we fell on it of one hundred and seventy miles. Remaining a few days on the main Snake River, we shaped our course north-west for sixty-four miles, till we fell on river Pagette or middle river; up which stream we proceeded to its source, a distance of one hundred and ten miles; then crossing over in a course nearly north, for some thirty miles, we fell on river Wuzer, down which we hunted until, at the distance of fifty miles, we again reached the main river. We found large numbers of beaver; but for want of canoes could do nothing. We then proceeded in a southerly direction till we made the great Snake camp of Ama-ketsa, where we had concluded the treaty of peace. During our survey of all these rivers, including that of Rivière aux Malades, we caught 1855 beaver.

Here let us take a retrospective view of a circumstance which occurred on leaving river Wuzer. As we were about to proceed to where the Snakes were numerous, I issued a certain quantity of ammunition to the hunters; cautioning them at the same time not to trade any of that essential article with the natives, nor to waste it, as our safety depended on it; and our stock was getting lower every day. The moment, however, the Iroquois and Half-breeds found themselves in possession of a sufficient supply, the plotting was revived; and on the very day we turned our backs on river Wuzer, they turned their backs on us: I only discovered their defection on reaching our encampment at night. John Grey, Martin, and ten others had lagged behind, with the intention of taking a different road to the one we had taken, and we were then too far apart to overtake them; so we continued on, in the hope that they might join us in a day or two.

On the fifth day, two of them with an Indian guide arrived at our camp with the news that the party had got into trouble with the Snakes; which did not surprise me. Our people had been exchanging horses, running races, and wrangling with the natives. Martin and a Snake having betted on their horses, the former lost the wager, when a bystander seeing Martin dissatisfied, went up to him, saying, "You do not know how to ride your horse to advantage; give him to me, and I will beat the Snake, and get back your ammunition again." Pleased at the proposal, Martin was simple enough to put his horse into the Indian's hands; when off started both the Snakes. Martin waited in vain: neither Snake nor horse ever returned. So, in addition to his ammunition, he lost his horse.

After this trick, our people and the Snakes quarrelled; when the latter, getting displeased, drove off four of their horses in broad daylight. To revenge this act, six of the whites, mounting their best horses, pursued; in order to get a-head and intercept the thieves at a narrow place where they had to pass, they took a short cut and got there first; then dismounting, they tied their horses at the edge of the woods; the men concealing themselves in the bush. The Indians not coming up at the time expected, the whites thought they might have taken another road; so they went further into the bush and set about cooking something for themselves before returning to camp, at the same time loosing their horses a little to feed. While they were thus employed, the Indians arrived, and seeing the horses, gave two or three yelps; the horses took fright and joined the other four, and the Indians drove them all before them; leaving their pursuers to return home on foot, with their saddles on their backs!

This was the story which the two men brought us, and they very pressingly asked for assistance. Thus separated, one half of us involved in a quarrel with the natives, and the other half in the vicinity of a formidable camp, requiring all our united strength,

I was for a moment at a loss what to do: to have sent a party back to their assistance, would have been exposing ourselves; to have left them without support, would have been sacrificing them. As there was little time for hesitation, I resolved at once on applying to our friend Pee-eye-em; but on reaching the Indian camp, I was mortified to find that Pee-eye-em had gone off to join his own people at a distance.

I had then nothing left but to apply to Ama-ketsa, the next in power; but he raised many objections, and said the guilty Indians were Bannatees, over whom he had no control. The temptation of a new gun, however, made the wily chief alter his tone, and he then undertook the mission: he recovered eight of the ten stolen horses, and arrived at our camp on the fourth day after his departure, bringing the whole party along with him. He had, however, managed, through cunning and under various pretences, to get from the Iroquois the remainder of their ammunition; but I had to overlook the sacrifice, and was contented to see us all together once more.

On Ama-ketsa's arrival with the party, he appeared very pleased and self-important; spoke in a laudatory strain of himself and the War-are-reekas generally, and dwelt particularly on their honesty and friendly disposition towards the whites; and thought we never could give him enough for the services he had rendered us. When I reproached my people for their conduct, the fault was shifted from one to another, and the Snakes blamed for all. We lost eight days' time, besides the risk we ran of more serious evils. Ama-ketsa strongly urged us to put up for a few days by the side of his camp; and although I did not like the situation, as much on account of the thoughtlessness of my own people, as from any apprehension of the Indians; yet, willing to show him a favour after the kind services he had done us, I complied with his request. So we encamped in a strong position, three-fourths surrounded by a bend of the river, having only our front to guard at the northern extremity of the great Snake camp.

We had no sooner got our camp in order than Ama-ketsa invited me to accompany him round the Indian camp; and in doing so, we had a train of at least five hundred followers! From the spot where we set out to the other end, was a distance of nearly five miles, and their tents were closely pitched on both sides of the river. I estimated the number of tents at about nine hundred of every description; and allowing only five persons to each, which was below the real number, we should have four thousand five hundred souls: and there might have been about half that number of horses about the place. There appeared to be but few armed with guns, in proportion to the number armed with bows and arrows.

This being the salmon season, Indians were flocking in from all quarters, and the quantity of salmon taken about this place alone, though this was not the great fish rendezvous, must have been immense: not less, perhaps, than twenty thousand daily!

Ama-ketsa's camp was ill-constructed for defence, and much exposed, had an enemy assailed it; but the division of labour was such, that every person seemed to be well occupied. Horse-racing, foot-racing, gambling, fishing, camp-making, wood-gathering, water-carrying, swimming, smoking, eating, sporting, and playing, went on in different parts of the Indian camp. The Snakes are not a lazy people; their camp was, however, very dirty, as all fish camps are. All classes we saw, with the exception of a few persons, were meanly clad, even for Indians; and very few of the men, and scarcely any women, were painted—a practice so prevalent among other tribes. But they were plump, oily, and sleek; with countenances rather dull than expressive; and appeared sociable and friendly among themselves.

During our ramble we had several opportunities of seeing and examining their native tobacco in its manufactured state. I purchased a gallon of it for a scalping knife; but I did not much like it: though as a substitute for tobacco, it is better than nothing. The natives use it from habit; but Ama-ketsa and several others smoked ours. We mixed with the people, stood and talked with them, and amused ourselves in examining their manner of doing their work; but not one of them ever said to us, "Will you eat?" We likewise saw them make their cricket and grasshopper broth; which appeared to me abominable and disgusting. We returned home in the evening very hungry, and with no favourable opinion of Snake hospitality.

We saw very few beaver among them; but at some distance from their camp, appearances were promising, so that my people were more anxious than prudent the following day, to set their traps. I had forbid them to do so, in order to avoid difficulties with the natives; but the chief assuring us that there would not be the least danger of the Indians either stealing or touching them, a few more traps were put in the water, and their success encouraged others to try their fortune. The first and second nights not one of the traps was touched; but on a subsequent trial no fewer than twelve were stolen: this sudden check to our proceedings opened our eyes to the character of the natives, and left us to judge how far their character was in accordance with the account the honest chief had given us. I spoke to Ama-ketsa on the subject, with the view of having our traps restored. The chief smiled, and made light of the matter; the other Indians taunted and jeered our people for making inquiries after their traps.

Soon after this discovery, I had to chastise one of them for attempting to steal a piece of rope out of our camp. These little grievances we winked at for some time, trying to check them gently, in order

ASSEMBLY OF THE WHITES. 105

to keep on good terms with Ama-ketsa and his people; but this conciliatory plan only encouraged them to assume a still greater degree of boldness. Thus matters went on until one evening a fellow picked up a bundle, and refusing to deliver it up, it was taken from him by force; he strung his bow, and threatened the man who had taken it from him, but was wise enough not to shoot.

On observing the daring aspect and conduct of the Indians, I assembled all my people together, and stated to them that I had known the character of these Indians for many years past, and that from their insolent behaviour of late it behoved us to keep a strict and vigilant eye on them; that it appeared evident to me they were seeking to intimidate us, and if they once thought they could succeed, they would rob us; and then they might attempt something else; but before they had gone too far, we must let them know that they could not encroach on our property with impunity. That united we were strong, and might teach them to respect us; whereas on the contrary, if we allowed them to take the footing they were assuming, we might regret having carried our forbearance too far. Twelve of our friends had already fallen victims to their barbarity; and what they had once done, they might attempt again, since they had stolen our traps, and had shown a disposition to set us at defiance!

I concluded by saying, we will go and seize just

so many of their horses as they have taken of our traps, and keep them as pledges, until they restore us our property: this will show them that we are not afraid of them. But my people demurred to this proposition: some said the Indians were too numerous; others, that we should all get killed. The Iroquois objected, because it would put an end to their traffic with the Indians; while those who had lost their traps, were, like myself, anxious to get them back, and to show that we were not to be trifled with. Some, however, called out, "We will go and take their horses, and after that fight them." I told them that we had not come on their lands to fight them, but to treat them kindly; yet in doing so, we must not allow the Indians to trample upon us. "Follow my advice," I said, "and there will be no fighting in the matter: make a bold stand in defence of our rights."

I then warned my men, that if any person exceeded his orders, he should be punished. At last, the whole party were convinced of the necessity of taking a decisive step to check the insolent tone of the Indians, and to pave the way for our getting away without loss or disgrace.

Arming ourselves, therefore, to the number of thirty-five, we sallied forth, seized, bridled, and brought into our camp ten of their horses; we then put everything in the best order for defence, knowing that this step would bring the matter to an issue. Two of the Indians being at our camp at the time, we counted out one hundred bullets before them, and poured them into our big gun in their presence, so that they might report the circumstance when they got to the Indian camp; we then sent them off with a message, that as soon as the Indians delivered up our traps, we would deliver up their horses.

When the two Indians had returned with the message to their camp, I instructed my people to have their arms in readiness, in such a position that each man could have his eye upon his gun, and could lay hold of it at a moment's warning; but to appear as careless as if nothing was expected. That if the Indians did come, as they certainly would, to claim their horses, and insisted on taking them, I would reason the matter with them; and when that failed, I would give the most forward of them a blow with my pipe stem, which was to be the signal for my people to act. The moment, therefore, the signal was given, the men were to shout according to Indian custom, seize, and make a demonstration with their arms; but were not to fire, until I had first set the example. During this time there was a great stir in the Indian camp; people were observed running to and fro, and we awaited the result with anxiety.

Not long after, we saw a procession of some fifty or sixty persons, all on foot and unarmed, advancing in a very orderly manner towards our camp; in front of which was placed our big gun, well loaded, pointed, and the match lit. My men were in the rear, whistling, singing, and apparently indifferent. On the Indians coming up to me and another man, who stood in front to receive them near to where the horses were tied, I drew a line of privilege, and made signs for them not to pass it. They, however, looked very angry, and observed the line with reluctance, so that I had to beckon to them several times before I was obeyed, or could make them understand. At last they made a sort of irregular halt.

I then made signs for the Indians to sit down; but they shook their heads. I asked where was Ama-ketsa; but got no satisfactory reply. One of the fellows immediately introduced the subject of the horses, in very fierce and insolent language; I however, to pacify him, and make friends, spoke kindly to them, and began to reason the matter, and explain it to them as well as I could; but the fellow already noticed, being more forward and daring than the rest, sneered at my argument, and at once laid hold of one of the horses by the halter, and endeavoured to take it away without further ceremony. I laid hold of the halter, in order to prevent him, and the fellow every now and then gave a tug to get the halter out of my hand; the others kept urging him on, and they were the more encouraged, seeing my people did not interfere; the latter were, however, on the alert, waiting impatiently for the signal, without the Indians being in the least aware of it. Beginning to get a little out of humour, I made signs to the Indians, that if he did not let go, I would knock him down; but, prompted no doubt by the strong party that backed him, and seeing no one with me, he disregarded my threat by giving another tug at the halter. I then struck him smartly on the side of the head with my pipe stem, and sent him reeling back among his companions; upon which my men sprang up, seized their arms, and gave a loud shout! The sudden act, with the terror conveyed by the cocking of so many guns, so surprised the Indians, that they lost all presence of mind; throwing their robes, garments, and all from them, they plunged headlong into the river, and swam with the current till out of danger, every now and then popping up their heads and diving again, like so many wild fowl! In less than a minute's time, there was not a soul of the embassy to be seen about our camp! Never was anything more decisive.

It may be satisfactory to the reader to know what kind of pipe stem it was that one could strike a heavy blow with. The pipe-bowls generally used, both by Indians and Indian traders, are made of stone, and are large and heavy; the stems resemble a walking-stick more than anything else, and they are generally of ash, and from two-and-a-half to three feet long.

We had intended removing camp the same day; but after what had happened, I thought it better to pass another day where we were, in order to give the Snakes as well as ourselves an opportunity of making up matters. Not a soul, however, came near us all that day afterwards, and we were at a loss to find out what was going on in the Snake camp. I therefore got about twenty of my men mounted on horseback, to take a turn round, in order to observe the movements of the Indians; but they having brought me word that the women were all employed in their usual duties, I felt satisfied.

During the following day, ten persons were observed making for our camp, who, on arrival, spread out a buffalo robe, on which was laid all our stolen traps! some whole, some broken into several pieces, which they had been flattening for knives; the whole rendered almost useless to us. Ama-ketsa, who had not been present at the affray of the preceding day, accompanied this party, and made a long and apparently earnest apology for the loss of our traps, and the misunderstanding that ensued; but he did not forget to exculpate his own people from all blame, laying the odium of the whole affair on the Bannatees. We knew the contrary: the War-are-reekas were the guilty parties, and perhaps Ama-ketsa himself was not altogether innocent; at least, some of his people said so. We, however, accepted the apology, and the traps, as they were; and delivering up all the horses, treated the chief with due honours, satisfied that the business ended so well.

The chief had no sooner returned to his camp with the horses, than a brisk trade was opened; the

Indians, men, women, and children, coming to us with as much confidence as if nothing had happened. On the next morning, while we were preparing to start, one of my men fell from his horse and broke his thigh; we, however, got it so set, as not to prevent our removal. Although everything wore the appearance of peace, yet I thought it necessary to take precautions, in order to avoid any trouble with the natives in passing their camp. I therefore appointed ten men mounted on horseback to go before, the camp followed in order after, while myself and twenty men brought up the rear; and all was peace and good order.

From the great Snake camp our course lay south, I purposing to take a sweep round the Snake Falls, with the view of trapping beaver and trying to get some accounts of our ten Iroquois. Fifty-seven beaver taken the first night, rewarded the toil of a long day's journey. At the Falls the concourse of natives resembled that at the Columbia Narrows (*Dalles des morts*) at this season of the year; but I was taught by our experience at Ama-ketsa's camp, not to put up near them; so we passed on. While at the Falls, the Indians told me that they had seen the Iroquois about a month before, and gave us to understand that they had got into difficulties with the Snakes, and were spending more time in hunting after women, than beaver.

From the Falls we continued our course south-east for about seventy miles, until we had reached the south end of a long range of high lands, which we called Point Turnagain; there we encamped on the 24th of August. This was the extent of our journey to the south: from that point we turned our faces towards home. Up to this date, we had travelled, since leaving the Flatheads, including trapping excursions apart from our regular journeys, 1110 miles; scouting excursions, watching our enemies, 490 miles; reconnoitring excursions for beaver, for practicable passes, and in search of new trapping ground, 530 miles; in addition to our daily journeys, which amounted to 1320 miles: making in the aggregate not less than 3450 miles!

From the mouth of river Wuzer, where we turned from the west to the south, the distance to Fort Nez Percés is not more than one hundred and eighty miles due west: a distance which might be travelled with horses in a week; and yet we had been travelling by the Spokane and Flathead road for upwards of seven months! At this stage of our journey, we had lost by casualties, chiefly from bad roads and severe weather, eighteen of our horses, and twenty-two of our steel traps; and had taken, exclusive of the Iroquois, 3880 beaver. Anticipating, therefore, a successful hunt from the Iroquois party, our prospects were still fair. From Point Turnagain, we took a wide range, and with tolerable success, until we again fell on Rivière aux Malades, according to our original plan.

On our way thither we passed over one of those

natural bridges so frequently noticed on former trips, the span of which was about thirty feet, the height twelve feet; and it appeared to be but one solid rock, through which the water had forced a passage, for under it passed a good stream, which flowed over a gravelly bottom. Following down the current, the water all of a sudden disappeared, making its way under ground, similar to the river Goddin: no water was then to be seen. We passed and repassed seven times over the ground, but saw nothing for a mile; when the water as suddenly burst out again, and flowed in a strong current, sufficiently deep to have carried a loaded boat on it! After following it for some distance, it disappeared; and we, taking another direction, saw it no more. In the last opening, we shot an otter and two musk rats. This subterraneous river flowed through one of the most delightful valleys I had ever seen, skirted on each side by gentle rising ranges of high lands, divided transversely between these ranges by descending rivulets, whose banks were lined with rows of bushes, as if planted by the hand of man. As we journeyed along, we passed several cold and hot springs. This enchanting vale I named the Garden of the Snake Country. It surpassed, both in beauty and fertility, the valley of the Wallamitte.

While journeying through this beautiful vale, which is some thirty miles in length, we were overtaken by a heavy deluge of rain (accompanied by the most fearful thunder and lightning), which drenched us to the skin, before we could get encamped: after which, having made a large fire out of doors, and while standing round it to dry ourselves, a flash of lightning passed as it were through the flame and almost blinded us, while the loud peal of thunder, instantaneously following, struck several of the party dumb for a moment. Three of the men were thrown down upon the ground, others upon their knees, myself and another man were forced out of the position in which we stood, to a distance of three or four feet. The whole camp remained for some time speechless. Within a short distance of us, the lightning struck a tree, setting it on fire. We had frequently this season been visited by heavy thunder, and much lightning is attracted to this mountainous quarter; but none of us had ever seen anything so terrific as in this place. We therefore named it the Valley of Lightning!

We now turn our attention to Rivière aux Malades. On reaching that stream we found beaver in considerable numbers: the first lift yielded forty-nine. The prospect before us was encouraging; but here a misfortune clouded our hopes, and made beaver a secondary consideration. After breakfast the second morning, a number of the people were taken ill; and the sickness becoming general throughout the camp, it struck me that there must have been something poisonous in our food or water. Not being able to discover anything, I began to inquire more particularly what each person had eaten that morning, and found that all those who had breakfasted on the fresh beaver taken out of the river were affected, whilst those who had eaten other food remained in good health.

Two hours had not elapsed before thirty-seven persons were seized with gripings and laid up. The sickness first showed itself in a pain about the kidneys, then in the stomach, and afterwards in the back of the neck and all the nerves; and at length the whole system became affected. The sufferers were almost speechless and motionless; having scarcely the power to stir, yet suffering great pain, with considerable froth about the mouth. I was seriously alarmed, for we had no medicine of any kind in our camp, nor scarcely time to have used it; so rapidly was the sickness increasing, that almost every soul in the camp, in the space of a few hours, was either affected with the disease, or panic-struck with fear!

The first thing I applied was gunpowder: throwing, therefore, a handful or two of it into a dish of warm water, and mixing it up, I made them drink strong doses of it; but it had little effect. I then tried a kettle of fat broth, mixed up and boiled with a handful or two of pepper which some of the people happened to have. I made them drink of that freely; and whether it was the fat or the pepper, I know not, but it soon gave relief. Some were only sick for part of the day; but others, owing perhaps to the quantity that they had eaten, were several days before they got over it; and some of them felt the effects of it for a month afterwards.

We then examined the flesh of the beaver, and found it much whiter and softer, and, the people who had eaten of it said, sweeter to the taste than the flesh of beaver generally. As there was no wood about the banks of the river, we supposed these animals must have lived on some root of a poisonous quality, which, although not strong enough to destroy them, yet was sufficiently deleterious to injure us: from this it was that I named this stream Rivière aux Malades.

Having trapped up the river to the place where we had left it, we then crossed over in order to trap some creeks in the mountains: here some of the horses had to swim, and several persons had a narrow escape of being drowned. On mustering on the opposite bank, I perceived at a considerable distance a Snake among the bushes, as if in the act of hunting for ground squirrels: beckoning to some of my people who were already mounted, and pointing to the individual, we set off at full speed to cut between him and the rocks, that we might get hold of him in order to learn something of the country we had to pass through. So intent was he on his business, that we were almost on him before he observed our approach; but the moment he saw us, he bent his bow, taking us for enemies.

Regardless of his bow and himself, we rushed in and laid hold of him; and on our dismounting from our horses, the poor creature let his bow and arrows fall to the ground, and stood speechless, and almost frightened to death.

We, however, mounted him behind one of the men, and carried him to our camp, where we treated him with every kindness, and at last, by means of our man Hackana, got him to speak a little. I ordered some beaver flesh to be set before him, putting some of the white or poisonous into one dish, and some of the good into another, purposely, to see if he knew the difference; but the two dishes were no sooner set before him, than he gave us to understand that the Indians invariably roast, but never boil, the white kind; telling us by signs, that it was bad, unless roasted.

We then entered at some length with our captive on the subject of their living, and how the Bannatees generally pass the winter; when he observed, —" We never want for plenty to eat, at all seasons. We often suffer from cold, but never from hunger. Our winter houses are always built among the rocks, and in the woods; and when the snows are deep, we kill as many deer as we please with our knives and spears, without our bows and arrows." To a question I put, he answered, "The Snakes never build their winter houses under ground." To other questions, he answered, "We can never venture in the open plains, for fear of the Blackfeet and Piegans, and for that reason never keep horses. Six of our people were killed by them this summer. Were we to live in large bands, we should easily be discovered." In reference to our road, he told us, that the country a-head was very rocky and bad, and that we could never make our way through it with horses. This miserable being, although the very picture of wretchedness, was far more intelligent and communicative than those we had got hold of on Reid's River. After passing a night with us, I gave him a knife, a small looking-glass, and a grain or two of vermilion; with which he went off highly delighted.

We continued our journey, winding through creeks and round rocks with great difficulty for eight days, until we had reached the extreme height of land between the sources of river Malade on the west, and Salmon River on the north. This ridge or height of land we passed on the 18th of September. The country was mountainous; and, a little to our right, was a towering peak, at least eight hundred feet higher than where we stood. Here, remaining a day to rest and refresh our jaded horses, I took a man along with me, in order to try and ascend this lofty peak. We set out at eight o'clock in the morning, and only got back at sun-set, so tired, that we could scarcely drag ourselves along. But the view we enjoyed repaid us well for our trouble. On the top of this height was six inches of newly-fallen snow, and a small circular pond of water about twenty feet in diameter. This height I named after our Governor, Mount Simpson; and the basin of water on its top, the Governor's Punch Bowl. No elevated height in this country can present a more interesting prospect than that viewed from the top of Mount Simpson: to the west, in particular, it is of a highly picturesque character. On looking towards the north, "How," said I to myself, " are we to pass here?" The doubt remained until I turned to view the quarter whence we had come; when, seeing it nearly as wild and rugged as country could be, it struck me, that since we had passed through the one, we might attempt the other.

We therefore left Mount Simpson, and descending into the narrow and unknown strath of Salmon River, shaped our course for Canoe Point, the place where we had left our beaver *en cache*. On getting down to the bottom of the valley, day was almost turned into night, so high were the mountains on each side of us; and in many places the view was so confined, that we could see nothing but the sky above and the rocks around us. Here the Salmon River, some three hundred and fifty miles long, was scarcely four feet wide; but many rills and creeks pouring into it from the adjacent rocks, soon swelled it into a river.

It appeared to us at first probable that no human being had ever trod in that path before; but we were soon undeceived, for we had not been many hours there, before my people, in going about their horses, found a pheasant pierced with a fresh arrow, and not yet dead; so, at the moment we were indulging that idea, the Indians might have been within fifty yards of us. As we advanced the valley widened, and the deer were seen feeding in numerous herds, and so tame, that we shot many of them without alighting from our horses, or going off the road after them; but it was not until the third day that we put a trap in the water, and seven beaver was all we got to reward us for so much labour.

At the distance of forty-seven miles from Mount Simpson, we entered on the west side of a fine stream, nearly as large as the main branch, being from thirty to forty yards broad, with deep water and a strong current. This place we called the Forks; the west branch, Bear River. On reaching the Forks, we observed at some distance the appearance of a ploughed field, and riding up towards it, found a large piece of ground more than four acres in extent, dug up and turned over. On getting to the spot, we observed no less than nine black and grizzly bears at work, rooting away. We immediately gave them chace, and, with the help of some twenty or thirty dogs, got four of them surrounded in front of a lofty and crumbling precipice, up which they endeavoured to make their escape; but the place being steep, and the stones and gravel loose, they made but slow progress, and the more so, as the dogs kept attacking them behind. Our horses, however, were so frightened, and became so restive, that we could not manage them, nor get them to approach the game; for no animal terrifies a horse more than a bear. At last, dismounting, we let the horses go, and fired at the bears, which were still scrambling to get up the rocky precipice; we brought three of the four down, but they had got so entangled and surrounded by dogs, that in killing the bears we killed seven of the dogs.

After our adventure, we set off on a trip of discovery up Bear River, for about thirty-four miles. The valley through which the river flowed was very pleasant, but became narrow as we advanced. Four inches of new snow were on the ground, and the ice was an inch thick. The weather was cold, and in those snowy regions indicated an early winter; yet we persevered in our pursuit of beaver, notwithstanding our course lay north, and we had yet before us some six or seven hundred miles before we reached our winter quarters. The wood on the banks of Bear River was only stunted willows, nor was there any other description in the neighbourhood fit for anything but fire; and but little even fit for that, if we except, now and then, a solitary pine not bigger than a good broom.

On rounding one of the many rocky points, we observed, some distance a-head of us, two animals frolicking in the water; on approaching the place, we discovered two black bears, and got so near as to shoot one of them in the water. While dragging it to shore, we noticed a beaver concealing itself in the shoal water, and this circumstance led us to ascertain why the bear should have been standing so long in the water. We found, by the number of tracks about the place, that the bears had been in pursuit of the beaver; there being but one deep hole where it could have swum under water and made its escape. At that place was artfully stationed the bear we had shot, while the other kept pursuing its object in the pool of water, where we found it, and it would have succeeded in killing the beaver but for our arrival.

Leaving six men to trap, I and another man returned to camp the second day, in order to examine the road by which we had to pass down the main river; but we found it so absolutely bad, that nothing but necessity compelled us to undertake it. After trapping for three days up Bear River, the six men returned to the camp, having killed one hundred and fifteen beaver. We then raised camp, left the Forks, and continued our route down the main branch of Salmon River.

About ten miles below the Forks, we entered a narrow and gloomy defile, where the mountains on each side closed in upon the river, between which the stream became confined like the water race of a mill, and shot through the narrow channel in a white foaming cascade, with the noise of thunder. Along the margin of the river in this dangerous place, the rocks and precipices descended almost perpendicularly to the water's edge, affording only a tortuous path some fifty or sixty feet above the water, in the face of the precipice. On this road we had advanced one day until we were abruptly stopped by a dangerous chasm where a piece of the hanging cliffs had slidden down, leaving a deep and yawning gap of some yards broad across the road, over which we could not pass. Here the horses being unable to get forward or backward, not having room to turn round, we had to use ropes to extricate several of them from their perilous situation; all hands calling out, "hold fast!" "hold fast!" While we in front were engaged in this no less dangerous than difficult task, the others, beginning at the rear, got the remainder turned back. We then retraced our steps about a mile, where we encamped. Here all our horses had to be tied, and we spent a restless night, under the apprehension that we should have to go back again to Mount Simpson and seek another pass to get clear of the mountains; which would have taken us, at that late season, some weeks and some hundred miles to accomplish.

After encamping, one of the men jocularly observed, that we ought to call the place "Hold fast!" and the name remained. On the next day, however, we resolved on attempting to cross the river; we examined it in several places, tried, and tried again, but failed the first day; the next, with difficulty, we crossed it to the opposite side. In this undertaking we drowned one of the horses, and lost four of our steel traps and about twenty-five beaver; and with the utmost difficulty we saved ourselves. Yet although we had accomplished the laborious task, we were not yet sure of getting through. From the crossing-place we wound among rocks and other obstructions for nearly two days, without advancing more than six or seven furlongs! At last, however, getting down again to the river, we got altogether clear of the defile on the eighth day. We reached Canoe Point at the end of a few hours' ride, after leaving the defile, and found the beaver we had left *en cache* safe.

At Canoe Point we remained for two days to rest and refresh our horses; for nearly one half of them were more or less lame, their hoofs being worn to the quick. Without being shod, no animals can stand the journeys through such a rugged country; and after one Snake expedition many of them are rendered useless. No less than twenty-seven of our horses had to be muffled about the feet with leather, which is at best but a temporary makeshift.

The season had now arrived when I was to send to meet the Iroquois who left us on the 16th of June, and on leaving Canoe Point I despatched six men to the Trois Têtons south of Goddin's River, the appointed rendezvous; while we proceeded on our journey in order to trap and make provisions for our voyage home, having appointed a place near the head waters of the Missouri where we were all to meet again. On the third day after starting, Jean Baptiste Bouché, one of the aged freemen, died in his sixty-ninth year: he had been ailing for some time, and for the last ten days had to be carried about on a litter. The deceased was a quiet, sober, and industrious man. We buried him in our camp, and burned the grave over, so that no enemy might disturb his remains; and near to the spot stands a friendly tree, bearing the inscription of his name, age, and the date of his death. As we advanced, we reached in a short time an immense herd of buffaloes, and commenced laying in a stock of provisions, until the men I had sent for the Iroquois should return.

While on the subject of buffalo, we may notice that there is perhaps not an animal that roams in this, or in the wilds of any other country, more fierce and formidable, than a buffalo bull during the rutting season: neither the Polar bear, nor the Bengal tiger, surpass that animal in ferocity. When not mortally wounded, buffalo turn upon man or horse; but when mortally wounded, they stand fiercely eyeing their assailant, until life ebbs away.

As we were travelling one day among a herd, we shot at a bull and wounded him severely—so much so, that he could neither run after us, nor from us; propping himself on his legs, therefore, he stood looking at us till we had fired ten balls through his body, now and then giving a shake of the head. Although he was apparently unable to stir, yet we kept at a respectful distance from him; for such is the agility of body and quickness of eye, and so hideous are the looks of buffalo, that we dared not for some time approach him: at last, one more bold than the rest went up and pushed the beast over;—he was dead! If not brought to the ground by the first or second shot, let the hunter be on his guard! The old bulls, when badly wounded and unable to pursue their assailant, prop themselves, as we have seen, and often stand in that position till dead; but the head of a wounded bull, while in an upright position, is invariably turned to his pursuer; so if the hunter be in doubt, let him change his position, to see if the bull changes his position also. The surest mark of his being mortally wounded and unable to stir, is, when he cannot turn his head round to his pursuer; in that case, you may safely walk up and throw him down.

The wild cow calves generally at one period, and that period later by a month than our tame cattle; then they all, as if with one accord, withdraw themselves from the mountains and rocks, and resort in large families to the valleys, where there is open ground, with small clumps of wood affording shelter and preservation; as there they can see the approach of an enemy from afar. The cows herd together in the centre, and the bulls graze in the distance: all in sight of each other.

The calving season is May, when the heat of the

sun is sufficiently strong for the preservation of their young in the open air; during which time the herd feeds round and round the place as if to defend the young calves from the approach of an enemy or from wolves. The resident Indian tribes seldom hunt or disturb the buffalo at this season, or before the first of July. The Indians often assured me, that, during the calving season, the bulls keep guard; and have been frequently known to assemble together, in order to keep at a distance any wolves, bears, or other enemies, that might attempt to approach the cows.

The men whom I had sent some time ago from Canoe Point in search of the Iroquois, had arrived, but had not met with them; they met with enemies instead, having a very narrow escape from a war party of the Blackfeet, who came upon them early one morning just as they were preparing to start; and so suddenly, that our people had to leave one of their horses as a prey to them. Fortunately for our people, the Indians were all on foot. I, however, lost no time in sending off, on the second day after their arrival, another party double in number to the first. They fortunately got safely back on the 14th of October, after an absence of ten days; bringing along with them not only the ten Iroquois, but seven American trappers likewise.

But they arrived trapless and beaverless; naked and destitute of almost everything; and in debt to the American trappers for having conveyed them to the Trois Têtons!

And this is their story. "We proceeded," said Old Pierre, "in a southerly direction, crossed over the main river, and struck into the interior to be out of the way of Indians; there we trapped with good success for nearly two months. At last some of the Snakes found us out, and Canataye-hare took one of their women for a wife, for whom he gave one of his horses. The Indians wished for another horse, but were refused; the wife deserted, and we changed to another place to avoid the Indians. There a war party fell on us, and robbed us of everything. We had nine hundred beaver, fifty-four steel traps, and twenty-seven horses: all of which, together with five of our guns, and nearly all our clothing, the Indians carried off! Naked and destitute as we then were, we set out on our way back; and on the third day after starting we fell in with the Americans; we promised them forty dollars to escort us back to Goddin's River, where we arrived the evening before the men you sent to meet us: and the Americans came along with us here. They had a good many beaver; but put them all *en cache* till they returned back." Such is the tale Old Pierre told me. When it was ended, I said, "Well, Pierre, what did I tell you at parting?" He held down his head, and said nothing.

I then questioned the Americans, who appeared

to be shrewd men: they confirmed part of the Iroquois' story. Smith, a very intelligent person, and who seemed to be the leading man among them, acknowledged to me that he had received one hundred and five beaver for escorting back the Iroquois to Goddin's River, although Pierre had not touched upon this circumstance at all: no two of them, however, told the story in the same way; nor did the Americans agree in their version of it, so that it appeared to me to be a piece of trickery from beginning to end. Some time after they had arrived, however, another story got into circulation; perhaps the true one. This story was not that they had been robbed, as Old Pierre had stated, but that while on their hunting ground, they fell in with the seven Americans noticed, who succeeded in seducing them to their side, under the pretext of giving them five dollars for every beaver-skin they might deliver at the Yellow Stone River, where the Americans had a trading-post; that with the view to profit by this contemplated speculation, they had left their furs *en cache* with those of the American party where they had been hunting, and had come back, not with the intention of remaining with us, but rather, as the story ran, to get what they could from us, and then to seduce their comrades to desert in a body with their furs to the Americans, as a party of them had already done in 1822: this story I had no difficulty in believing.

I, however, thought it best not to say that I either

heard or believed this last story; at the same time I tried to find out the truth of it: I knew there must be some knavery going on between the Americans and the Iroquois, from the constant intercourse that existed between them. I, however, took such steps as would most effectually prevent the possibility of their being able to carry their intentions into effect. It aided my plans greatly that the enemy kept hovering about, and I of course exaggerated the danger, making it a pretext for doubling the watch by night, and remaining on guard myself; but, in truth, it was to prevent either the Iroquois or the Americans from taking any undue advantage of us: in the meantime I daily forced our march to get the nearer to home.

The measures we adopted succeeded so well, that the Americans at last gave up the idea, preferring the protection of our camp to the risk of turning back.

CHAPTER XIII.

Report—Enemies in sight—The agreeable mistake—The ten Nez Percés—Their story—Suspicious defile—Reconnoitring party—Enemies discovered—The pursuit—A hard ride—The hiding-place—Gathering the spoil—The peace-offering—Suspicious party—Anxieties of the whites—The surprise—The stolen horses—The thieves caught—Indians mute—Nez Percés reproved—Thieves in custody—Return to camp—The court-martial—Wild fowl—Sporting—Hard shooting—World of game—The mourning scene—The snowy mountain—Change of scenery—Valley of Troubles again—Ice and snow—Cold travelling—Hell's Gates—A horse drowned—Arrive at Flathead house—Fruits of the expedition—Remarks—Yankee enterprise—New plan proposed—The men—Contemplated results—Depôt for the returns—Wants created—Inland position—Speculation—Sketch of the Snake people—Position of the Snakes—Their courage—Snake language.

WE had no sooner done with the adventures of our absent trappers than the people were thrown into confusion by a report that enemies were approaching the camp. And although such reports were not unfrequent, they never failed to create a momentary thrill, whenever a sudden alarm was given. This is unavoidable.

We prepared to receive the comers either as

friends or foes, but were soon agreeably relieved from our fears, by finding that they were our friends, the Nez Percés. These poor weather-beaten wanderers, only ten in number, passed the night with us, and amused us with recounting their wild adventures. We shall give the reader their own simple story.

"When we left our own country, about three months ago," said they, "our object was to fall in with the whites in the Snake country. We were then seventeen in number, and on foot, the better to conceal ourselves from the enemy. We intended to have stolen horses for ourselves from the Blackfeet had an opportunity offered, in revenge for those they had taken from us at Hell's Gates in the spring. One turned back, and in crossing a rocky defile at the head waters of the Missouri, we were discovered, and waylaid by the Blackfeet; six were killed in that unfortunate affray, and the rest of us had a very narrow escape, only getting clear of the enemy by escaping in the dark. From that time we only travelled at night. Despairing of meeting the whites, and seeing the buffalo moving to and fro, we knew that there must be enemies lurking about, and had to hide ourselves; we suffered greatly from hunger and thirst, and had almost given up any hopes of getting back to our own country again, when all at once we perceived the whites coming, whom at first we took for a large war-party."

After they had related the story of their

troubles, they began to mourn for their unfortunate relations who were killed in the defile; then they appeared overjoyed at getting under the protection of the whites, and vowed vengeance against the Blackfeet.

The Nez Percés telling us that there were enemies lurking about, and we having a suspicious defile to pass, I thought it well to have the place examined before raising camp the next day. This being settled, I took five of the Indians along with us, and we set off to the number of six-and-thirty persons, taking care to have two of the Americans and the most troublesome of my own men among the party. Just as we had got the bad part examined, and reached the other side, we perceived, at a long distance off, a number of moving objects making for the mountains; but whether men or deer we could not ascertain. Losing no time, however, we resolved on giving chace, and therefore set off at full speed to get between the objects we saw and the woods they seemed to be making for. Before we had advanced far, we were satisfied that the objects were men and not deer; which made us quicken our steps.

The Indians, on discovering us, began to quicken their pace, and make for a hiding-place. We at the same time advanced at full speed. The match was warmly contested; but the Indians won the race by a short distance, and got to the bush before we could reach them. In their hurry, however, they had thrown away everything that encumbered them, robes, shoes, and some of them even their bows and arrows; and yet after all, we had got near enough to have fired upon the last of them before they got under cover, had we been so disposed. Immediately on getting to the bush where the Indians had taken shelter, we dismounted, and invited them to come out of the woods and smoke with us, assuring them that we were their friends; but they answered, "Come in here and smoke with us: we are your friends." We then sat down on a little rising ground close to the Indians, to rest our horses a little, for we had given them a good heating; keeping all the time in talk with the Indians. They gave us to understand that they were Crows, the name of a tribe on the Missouri; but although they spoke to us in that language, the impression on our minds was, that they were Blackfeet, and we told them so; this they denied, on account, no doubt, of having killed the Nez Percés, some of whom they now saw with us.

Some of the people in the meantime went and gathered together what things the Indians in their hurry threw away; namely, sixteen buffalo robes, six dressed skins, fifty-two pairs of mocassins, and two quivers full of bows and arrows; all of which we laid in a pile, telling the Indians we did not wish to injure them, nor take away anything belonging to them. Then taking a piece of tobacco we stuck it on a forked stick at the edge of the bush, for them to smoke after our departure. To questions we put, they denied having seen the six men sent to river Goddin, or the horse which they had lost; they said there were several parties of Blackfeet and Piegans both, not far off; that they themselves had been looking for some of their absent friends, but were now on their way back to their own country. We then prepared to return, but had some difficulty in preventing the Nez Percés from taking the spoil we had picked up, and also from firing on the Indians in the bush; however, I told them that, since they were with the whites, and put themselves under our protection, they must do as we did; but that if they were bent on revenge, they might stop where they were until we had gone away, and then settle matters as they might think proper.

As we were in the act of mounting our horses to return, we perceived at a distance the appearance of a crowd of men and horses, following the track by which the Indians had come, and making straight for us. From their appearance at a distance they seemed very numerous, and taking them for another war-party, we considered ourselves between two fires. Not wishing, however, to run off, we examined a small point of the woods near to the Indians, where we could retreat in case of being too hard pressed; we then secured our horses, under a guard of ten men, while the other twenty-six, with their guns ready, awaited the arrival of the suspicious party.

As soon as we had observed them, we discovered the party to consist of four men only, driving, however, a large band of horses before them; when they had got within a few hundred yards of us they made a halt, which they had no sooner done, than I ordered twenty of my men to remain where they were, as a guard on the Indians, while I and the other fifteen set off to meet, and see who the new comers were. On getting up to them, what was our surprise on finding forty-three of our own horses, and also the one taken from my men on their trip to the trappers; all of which the four villains had stolen and were driving before them.

On our approach the thieves immediately fled; we pursued, and got hold of three of them, the fourth making his escape among the rocks. They belonged to the party in the bush. Our first impression was to have punished the offenders on the spot; but reflecting a little that there might have been other horses stolen, we kept them as hostages, to see how things would end. I therefore carried them back to our camp.

After the bustle was over, we secured the thieves, and collected all our horses; then returning to the place where I had left the twenty men to guard the Indians, we tried to re-open a communication with them. But they would not speak a word to us, although they spoke to each other in our hearing. So we took all the property we had picked up belonging to them, also the tobacco I had left for them to smoke, together with the three prisoners, and returned to our camp; where we arrived late, after a hard day's work.

On reaching the camp, we were told that the stolen horses had not been missed until late in the afternoon, although they must have been driven off soon after we started in the morning: two parties had been in pursuit, but none of them happened to fall on their trail; and had they escaped us, we never should have seen one of them. The rest of our horses being safe, we held a court-martial on the three criminals, when the sentence pronounced by every voice in the camp, with the exception of myself and two others, was to have them shot; but after giving them a good fright, I managed to procure their escape the following day. Raising camp, therefore, we commenced our journey through the defile we had examined the day before, taking the condemned criminals with us as prisoners. With a view of preventing the sentence from being put into execution, I selected some men on whom I could depend, and delivered the criminals into their hands, with strict orders to let them go while passing through the defile. The Nez Percés, Iroquois, and I, for obvious reasons, went on ahead, and all ended as I wished.

I was very happy that the miserable wretches got off with their lives, for depriving them of life would have done us no good, neither would it have checked horse-stealing in those barbarous places.

Having once more got out of our troubles with

the natives, we pursued our homeward journey with great eagerness, as the cold of winter was closely pressing us in the rear. We, however, continued trapping and hunting, in order to make up, in some degree, for the loss we had sustained by the misconduct of the Iroquois.

It not unfrequently happened, however, that natural causes operated against us; for we had to break the ice in order to relieve our traps almost every morning; nor was this all: the immense flocks of wild fowl which hovered about the numberless rivulets and pools at the head-waters of the Missouri and other minor rivers, in their passage to a warmer climate, tempted even the most industrious among us to forego the more profitable pursuit of trapping for the gratification of shooting geese and ducks. Much time was, therefore, lost, and much ammunition spent, to little purpose.

But this superabundance of wild fowl was not the only attraction to divert our attention. We were, at the same time, surrounded on all sides by herds of buffalo, deer, moose, and elk, as well as grouse, pheasants, and rabbits. From morning to night, therefore, scarcely anything else was to be heard about our camp but the sound of guns and the cries of wild fowl and other animals.

As we journeyed among the rocks and defiles, the Nez Percés took us a little out of our way, and showed us the spot where their six companions had fallen a sacrifice to the fury of their enemies; and also the place where the Blackfeet who had killed them lay in ambush. That one of them escaped with their lives was a matter of wonder to us. These victims had, according to Indian custom, been all scalped, cut to pieces, and their limbs strewed about the place. On arriving at the fatal spot, the poor fellows wrought themselves into a frantic state of mourning, tearing their hair, cutting their flesh, and howling like wild beasts for some time; then gathering up the remains of the dead, they buried them at a distance.

After a few days' hard travelling, with more or less success in the way of hunting, we encamped at the foot of the celebrated mountain where we had spent so much anxious labour in the spring, cutting our road of eighteen miles long through a mass of snow from eight to ten feet deep. The scene was wholly changed: the mountain, then so terrific, was now the reverse; all the old snow had been swept away by the summer heat. A sprinkling of new-fallen snow, not six inches deep, was all that concealed the features of the surface from the eye; and the next day, in six hours' time, we crossed it without ever alighting from our horses. We encamped in the Valley of Troubles, equally celebrated as being our prison for thirty-five days; but its appearance at this season, although still wrapped in the white mantle of snow, was more cheering than it was in the spring. At this time we could smile with content, inasmuch as every step put our difficulties further behind us. Here we set our traps, but only obtaining two otters, and no beaver, our trapping ceased.

Soon after we had encamped, fresh tracks, supposed to be those of enemies, were discovered; which made me remark that there was no passing that place without troubles. We therefore doubled the guard on our camp and horses; but next morning all was safe. Raising camp, therefore, we bade farewell to the Valley of Troubles, continued our march, and visited the Ram's Head again. Our road was encumbered with ice and snow, over which we had to make our way with difficulty till we reached Hell's Gates. Nor at that place were our troubles diminished; for the river which we had to cross was partially frozen over with ice, both solid and drift, and, with our utmost care, one of our horses was drowned, and two of our men were nearly sharing its fate.

Hell's Gates being now behind us, as well as our dreaded enemies, we looked upon the danger and troubles of the journey as ended. We quickened our pace, and every step now became more and more cheering, until the termination of our journey at Flathead House, which we reached at the end of November. As the reader may wish to know the extent of our success in the object of our pursuit, after all our toils, I may say that, all things considered, our returns were the most profitable ever brought from the Snake country in one

FRUITS OF THE EXPEDITION.

year; amounting to 5000 beaver, exclusive of other peltries. I had the satisfaction of receiving, from Governor Simpson, a letter of thanks on the success of the expedition. This brings our Snake adventures to a close.

The most prominent defects of the present trapping system and Snake expeditions are, first, the quality of the hands employed; secondly, the equipping depôt; and thirdly, the mode of regulating the annual trips. In the selection of men for a Snake expedition, it has always been customary, heretofore, to collect all the refuse about the different establishments, merely with a view, it would appear, to make up numbers:—all the lazy, cross-grained, and objectionable among the engaged class; the superannuated, infirm, and backsliding freemen; the wayward half-breed, the ignorant native; and, last of all, and worst of all, the plotting and faithless Iroquois:—taking it for granted that, if conducted by an experienced leader, all would go on well.

So long as Spokane House is made the starting point, so long will the Snake business be a loss. The distance is too great; and experience has proved that in proportion to the distance, so are the risks and disappointments. Now we have already pointed out the locality of Spokane House; but, that its unfitness may, if possible, be convincing to all, we shall make such further remarks as will set the question at rest for ever. The distance, then, from Nez Percés, by Spokane House, to reach the Snake country, subjects the trapper to a laborious journey of 690 miles more than he would be subject to by starting direct from Nez Percés: the roads are worse, and the natives more hostile. The distance from Nez Percés to Oakanazan is 200 miles north; from Oakanazan to Spokane House, 140 miles east; from Spokane House to the Flatheads, 170 miles east by south; and from the Flatheads to the Valley of Troubles, 180 miles south. These distances are, perhaps, not critically correct, but they are near the truth. The Valley of Troubles we consider to be the parallel of Nez Percés, lying in the direction of almost due east: for when the trapper is there, he is not nearer to the Snake country than he was when at Nez Percés, the point from whence he started.

As this distance cannot be performed in winter, it has to be travelled in the spring and fall of the year, and at the time the trapper ought to be engaged in his field of chase: indeed, he ought to be on his hunting-ground all the year round.

And in the annual trips also, the whole body of trappers abandoning their hunting-ground every autumn, and returning thither every spring, is discouraging: it subjects them to severe trials, unnecessary expense, loss of time, and not unfrequently loss of lives, from the danger of the route. Their short visits and casual sojournings never allow them either time or opportunity to make good hunts, or to form a community of interests with the natives. Everything, therefore, essential to both parties, in as far as regards the interest of the trader or the social improvement of the Indians, is, and has always been, lost sight of by the mistaken policy of the whites.

Let the reader turn back and take a glance at Point Turnagain, and there he will find that we had to commence our homeward journey on the 24th of August, at the very time we ought to have been preparing for commencing our fall hunts; and then we only got to the Flatheads on the ice and snows of winter.

Having briefly stated, and I hope satisfactorily, some of the evils resulting from the present system, I now come to propose the remedy. I have advocated the plan, although without success, for the last ten years; and the more I have seen of the country and its resources, the more I am convinced of its proving successful.

Our southern and more enterprising neighbours have not lost sight of the advantages thus offered them, but continue year after year advancing with hasty strides, scouring the country, and carrying off the cream of the trade; and if we do not speedily bestir ourselves, the Yankees will reap all the advantages of our discoveries. While our great men west of the mountains, as we have often stated, look on with a degree of supineness unparalleled in former days; contenting themselves with the fabulous tales of others, and too often listening to the unfavourable side of things: as is manifest from their adherence to the old system. These dignitaries no sooner attain what they consider the last step in promotion's ladder, than they sink down at once into indolence and spend the remainder of their probationary term at ease; as if promotion quenched ambition and lulled the passion of enterprise to sleep: this has given rise to a common saying in this country, that one chief clerk is worth two chief traders, and one chief trader is worth two chief factors. Nor is the remark perhaps destitute of truth, for during the eight years the Snake country had been under the North-West Company, and the four years it has now been subject to the Hudson's Bay Company, neither a Bourgeois of the former, nor a titled functionary of the latter, has ever yet set a foot in that quarter to see and judge for himself.

Now to my plan. First, I hold Fort Nez Percés to be the most eligible starting point for the trade of the Snake country, so long as the Columbia River is the port of transportation; for it possesses more advantages and is liable to fewer objections than any other.

Taking Nez Percés as the starting point in future, I would next advert to what may be called the mainspring of all the machinery—the kind of trappers most fitted to the business of the Snake country. Good, steady men of character, thrifty and persevering, are the men required, no matter to what class or country they may belong: such hands can always be depended upon; their own interest would be a guarantee for their good conduct. In short, such men as the general run of servants throughout the country are; or I would say the more steady and better class of them.

These men would not, however, be denominated freemen; for in this country there is something depraved in the word freedom. They should be engaged for three or five years; and once on their field of chase, there remain stationary, for the purpose of trapping beaver at all seasons of the year, or such other duties as might be found necessary. With such men as we have described, and under such regulations, there would be little doubt as to a successful issue. Besides, we possess advantages now which we did not before: we know the country, we know the natives, we know the best hunting-grounds, and we are acquainted with the best roads, the difficulties, the dangers, the wants of the natives, and the requisite articles for carrying on the trade to the best advantage. In fact, we know almost everything connected with the business.

The trappers remaining on their trapping-ground all the year round, could avail themselves, under an active and intelligent conductor, of all the advantages the country possesses; and they would have this additional advantage, that in conveying their furs to Fort Nez Percés, they would do so, not as formerly at the expense of their spring or fall hunt, but in the middle of summer, when there is no hunting going on. In the heat of summer, the beaver is always of an inferior quality, and then all trapping ceases for a certain time. This season would also be the time when the hostile tribes would be absent, either hunting the buffalo or at war, and consequently removed out of the way of the whites; so that the route would be clear and the roads safe.

In the Snake country there is a field large enough and rich enough for one hundred trappers, for a quarter of a century to come. But I will go upon a smaller scale, and begin the business on this new plan, with the same number as was employed formerly; say fifty, with five extra hands as a camp guard. Now in my late expedition, with the medley of fifty-five men, which composed my party at first, there were only twenty-eight of the number trappers; some even of that number very indifferent, and badly provided with traps, having only, on an average, five each, when they ought to have had double that number on such long journeys. As we got a few skins from the Iroquois before they left the party and after they joined it again, and as I wish to make my calculations upon as fair a scale as possible, I shall say that I only lost the hunts of eight, leaving my number of actual trappers just twenty; yet they averaged

250 beaver each. Now if twenty trappers produce 5000 beaver in a given time, a simple question in the rule of three will tell us that fifty trappers ought to produce 12,500 beaver in the same time. And if we calculate upon the quality of the hands, and the superior advantages they would possess, in time as well as in everything else, we ought reasonably to anticipate at least one-third more from them; the supply being inexhaustible.

But it is not on a starting point, nor on the trappers alone, that the success of the business on the improved system will chiefly depend; we must have a trading establishment in the Snake country likewise, to serve as a rallying point for all hands, where they could assemble at stated periods. This establishment would serve as a depôt for the returns, where they would remain in safety, from time to time, to wait the season of transportation; and would relieve the hunters from the risk of carrying about their beaver, on weak and jaded horses, all the year round; or of making *câches*, a practice never free from more or less risk.

The advantages, however, of an establishment of this kind can only be fully appreciated by those conversant with the more minute details of the business.

Now let us see how far an establishment of this kind would benefit the natives, or be favourable to the trade generally. The Snakes have invited us often to form an establishment among them.

They are often engaged in a defensive war; they have no traders, consequently they are under every disadvantage. Not an hour, therefore, but they would be teasing us for something: one would want a gun—a gun requires ammunition; and what one would be in want of, so would another, so would all. In short, they want everything, for they have nothing; and by the time we could supply them with all their wants, we should be enriched and they would be civilised. They have promised us every protection and every encouragement, and so anxious are they to obtain the boon, that their promises were unbounded, and we left them with regret. The natives are numerous, beaver plentiful, and a growing desire to possess our toys and trinkets would soon make them industrious hunters. On the whole, but few heavy articles would be required; as clothing they do not want. Vermilion, beads, and buttons, axes, knives, awls, and needles, are the articles most desired by them, next to their warlike implements. A blacksmith, and a few hundred weight of iron attached to the establishment, would alone be worth a whole trapping expedition.

The establishment would be a simple stockaded fort or trading post; the erection of which would cost next to nothing, for the trappers, during the idle season, would be amply sufficient to do all the work necessary, as is customary in other parts of the country. It might or might not be a permanent establishment: it might be here this year, and removed to the distance of a hundred miles the next, as occasion required; it being chiefly intended as a stronghold for the benefit of the trappers, as well as for the convenience of trading with the natives. At the same time, the trappers would, in a more or less degree, by their presence in the vicinity, serve as a guard for its protection.

And a post once established among them, the last but not the least essential part of this simple plan of improvement is to abolish altogether the transportation of property, either furs or merchandise, by horses, and avail ourselves of the superior advantages offered by water communication; it having been satisfactorily proved, in the spring of 1819, by Mr. M'Kenzie, that the navigation of the south branch is perfectly practicable.

The expenses, therefore, both as to men and merchandise, of this post, exclusive of the hunters, would be but a mere trifle annually; and it would be well worth the experiment, for the security and advantages it would afford to the trappers alone. But I will now view it solely in the light of a trading post: as such, the Indians would flock to it from all quarters, from interest as well as curiosity; and the spirit of emulation would be kindled among a people long neglected. All the Snakes would become purchasers, and every purchaser would have to become a beaver hunter. But let us not raise our expectations too high. The Snakes are not now beaver hunters; but there is no doubt that they would, like other Indians, soon become so, on the introduction of whites among them; as the possession of one article would create a desire to possess another: and in the meantime their numbers would make up for their unskilfulness.

Keeping these points in view, I would notice that there are 36,000 souls in the Snake country; and allowing six to a family, that would give 6000 families. Now my anticipations would not surely be stretched beyond moderation, in expecting two beaver skins from each family, even for the first year; equal to 12,000 beaver. And should the trappers realise our expectations, in doing their duty, both results put together would yield 24,500 beaver annually. That ought, according to the new system, to be the returns of the Snake country in future; and might have been the returns for years past, had men been alive to their own interests.

I have endeavoured to make myself understood, by developing the outline of the plan as plainly on paper as it appears in all its parts practicable to me. But as I have not calculated the more minute details of all the expenses which this branch of the trade would cost, nor perhaps made all due allowances for contingencies (which could not well be done), I dare not affirm what the annual profits would be; but were I to hazard an opinion I should estimate the clear gain at not less than ten thousand pounds sterling per annum.

Having presented the reader with a sketch of my plan for improving the trade of the Snake country, I shall next make a few remarks on the condition of the natives, as we found them; and finally, conclude with a brief specimen of their language.

Although I have divided the great Snake nation into three separate sections, the distinction cannot be considered very definite, since they invariably mix and intermarry with each other. Besides, they all seem to be governed by the same laws: their manners, their feelings, and their principal habits are likewise the same. Taking them altogether then, as a family of the human race, they have been considered and represented as rather a dull and degraded people, diminutive in size, weak in intellect, and wanting in courage. And this opinion is very probable to a casual observer at first sight, or when seen in small numbers; for their apparent timidity, grave, and reserved habits, give them an air of stupidity.

An intimate knowledge of the Snake character will, however, place them on an equal footing with those of other kindred nations, either east or west of the mountains, both in respect to their mental faculties and moral attributes. The Snakes, from their inland position, have seldom been visited by the whites; nor was it until the Oregon territory began to attract public attention, and stimulate a spirit of inquiry into the regions of the far west, that the Snakes, as a nation, became generally known. Nor had traders ever penetrated into that distant wilderness; so that they remained, until lately, in their primeval simplicity. Meanwhile they have been surrounded on all sides by powerful and warlike nations, which nations have, for nearly a century past, been frequented by traders, and consequently, all that time, furnished with fire-arms and other weapons of war; to the great annoyance and almost ruin of the poor and defenceless Snakes, who have had to defend their country and protect themselves with the simple bow and arrow, against the destructive missiles of their numerous enemies.

Hence it was that the Blackfeet, the Piegans, and other tribes east of the mountains, and, at a later period, those on the Columbia likewise, have made the Snake country the theatre of war; and hence the Snakes, from their unarmed and defenceless state, have been stigmatised as a dastardly race unskilled in the art of war. Thus it is that so many slaves, scalps, and other barbarous trophies have, from time to time, been taken from them and carried off; and these occasional successes have always been represented to their disadvantage, without, however, once assigning the real cause—the unequal combat which they carried on. But arm the Snakes, and put them upon an equal footing with their adversaries, and I will venture to say, from what I have seen of them, that few Indians surpass them in boldness or moral courage: my only wonder is, that they have been able, under so many discouraging circumstances, to exist as a nation, and preserve their freedom and independence so long.

SNAKE LANGUAGE.

One	Shameats.
Two	Watts.
Three	Payatahop.
Four	Whatsaw.
Five	Mannee.
Ten	Equamoaks.
Beaver	Chinish.
Camp	Cannought.
Whites	Tabeboo.
Indians	Shoshonee.
Good	Tisand.
Bad	Quoitsand.
Water	Paw.
River	Parrow.
Salmon	Agaitah.
Mountain	Tiebit.
Cross over	Mairmaw.
Far off	Mirancoineat.
Near to	Steesheets.
Sun	Sabeigh.
Moon	Mayhow.
Night	E' Oh.

SNAKE LANGUAGE.

Sleep	Equamamequa.
Tongue	Johumby.
Morning	Eyesequittaw.
Guard	Tecome.
Iron	Wyesk.
Nose	Mop.
Eyes	Poetaill.
Ears	Eatate.
Hand	Mawze.
Hair	Bauks.
Dog	Sherry.
Horse	Warack.
Buffalo	Pishish.
Blanket	Cutto.
Knife	Wheat.
Large	Buyap.
Small	Eyoutassteaw.
Fat	Payuhoope.
Poor	Cowa.
Gun	Kooreackack.
House	Nobill.
Thief	Kaysleonand.
Again	Tieass tiass.
Fear	Pyeanttea.
Yes	Kaick.
No	Waypo.
Work	Gouree.

* It is now a quarter of a century, or more, since the discussion of the trade of the Snake country occupied the attention of fur-traders. In those days it was, indeed, a question of some importance, and worth contending for; but that importance was at the time, as the reader must be aware, overlooked, or at least never taken advantage of, by the English traders then in the country; and it is now regarded by those who know no better as a tale twice told—of little value. True, the lapse of years have

brought about many changes, and, among others, the country itself may be said to have changed masters; nevertheless, up to the present day it has not diminished in riches nor in importance to fur-traders. And however I may regret that my remarks were not made public at the time I first wrote, I am not on that account to look on things past and gone as utterly useless; nor ought what I have said to be considered as out of place, inasmuch as it illustrates the history of a bygone period. I can state with undiminished confidence, that the Snake country towards the Rocky Mountains is, and will be, rich in furs for some generations to come, and full of interest to men of enterprise. Indeed, the dangers by which it was then, and still is, in a more or less degree, surrounded, will always tend to preserve the furs in that inland quarter. Small trapping parties can never ruin the country, but they will ruin themselves. It is only strong and formidable parties that can ever inherit these riches; and now that the Americans are fast spreading themselves in that direction, these mines of wealth will not be overlooked, nor the long-neglected natives, we trust, be allowed to remain much longer in darkness and idolatry.

CHAPTER XIV.

Dawn of education on the Oregon—Speech of a Kootanais chief—The farewell—Juvenile adventurers—Result—Flathead River—The Forks—Interview—Party set out for the Rocky Mountains—Parting scene—Facilities—Bold undertaking—View of the subject—Kettle Falls—Fort Colville—Remarks—Gloomy place—Petit Dalles—Some account of the place—Islands—A boat in jeopardy—Kootanais River—Stony barrier—Desolation—No Indians—No animals—First lake—Extent—Scenery—The wounded Indian—Jealousy in the wilderness—New-fashioned canoes—Link between the lakes—Upper lake—Sudden appearance of an Indian—Chief of the Sinatcheggs—His story—Some account of his country and people—The deception—Length of upper lake—Some account of the country—The child—Peace-offering—The wretched flock—Gloomy aspect—Perilous navigation—The ideal city—M'Kenzie's River—Dalles des Morts—Seat of desolation—Natural curiosity—Moisture—Castle-rock ores—Transparent substances—A man in a gold mine—Ross's River—Cataract creeks—The circus—Diamond creek—Brilliant objects—Beaver islands—M'Millan's River—Landscape in confusion—Belle Vue point—Deceitful windings—The steersman's warning—Canoe River—Northernmost point of Columbia—Portage River—Main branch—Length of north branch—Land on Portage point—Columbia voyage concluded.

HAVING closed my remarks on the Snake country, I resume my narrative. The reader will remember that we had reached the Flatheads at the end of November. I passed the winter in charge there; and during my residence was desired by Governor Simpson to try and procure two Indian boys from their relations, for the purpose of being educated at Red River Colony. This was a new and promising feature in the policy of the place—it was the dawn of a brighter day west of the mountains, and ought long to be remembered with gratitude.

These natives, notwithstanding their aversion to part with their children—and particularly so on this occasion, it being the first proposal that had ever been made to them by the whites, for their children to leave their native country, either for education or any other purpose—had so much confidence that, after a council or two had sat, the chiefs not only complied with the request, but, as a more striking example of their willingness, agreed to let two of their own children avail themselves of the proffered boon, whom they without hesitation delivered up to me.

When the business was over, with all the ceremony attending it, the father of one of the boys got up and made an harangue:—"You see," said he to me, "we have given you our children: not our servants, or our slaves, but our own children;" striking at the same time one hand on his left breast, and with the other pointing to one of his wives, the mother of the boy. "We have given you our hearts—our children are our hearts; but bring them back again to us before they become white men—we wish to see them once more Indians—and after that, you can make them white men, if you like. But let them not get sick, nor die: if they get sick, we shall get sick; if they die, we shall die. Take them; they are now yours." The chief then sat down, when all present broke out into lamentations; after which the chiefs rose, and putting the boys' hands into mine, we parted. The scene was very affecting, and I felt great regret at their parting.

One of the boys was the son of a Kootanais chief, and named by us Pelly, after the Governor of the Hudson's Bay Company; the other was a son of one of the Spokane chiefs, and we called him Garry, after one of the Directors; they were about ten or twelve years old, both fine promising youths of equal age. As it is not likely we shall be recurring to this circumstance again, we may mention that the boys reached their destination, and were educated at the Missionary School. At the end of two or three years, however, Kootanais Pelly, after making considerable progress in learning, died; some years afterwards, Spokane Garry returned back to his own country with a good English education, and spoke our language fluently. These were the first Indians belonging to the Oregon territory ever taught to read and write; for which the praise is due to Governor Simpson.*

We return to our subject. Leaving Flathead

* This boy, Spokane Garry, did not realise the expectations entertained of him on his return to his countrymen.—See Sir Geo. Simpson's "Narrative," page 144.

House early in the spring, with the furs of the post and the Snake returns, which had of necessity to pass the winter at that place, we commenced our voyage down Flathead River. This takes a long time on account of the intricate navigation; that river being shoal, and full of rapids, all the way down to Lake Callispellum—a small sheet of water so called after the tribe of that name, and through which the river passes. A little beyond the west end of the lake, we leave Flathead River altogether, as it continues its course to the right; our road led to the left, that we might avail ourselves of the portage (an overland carriage of some thirty miles) to Spokane House, and from thence by the same mode of conveyance to the Forks or mouth of Spokane River. There we arrived, after a voyage of 240 miles, on the 12th April, 1825.

The reader will here notice that there is no water communication leading either to or from Spokane House, navigable for any craft larger than an Indian canoe. Here I had the honour of an interview with Governor Simpson, for the first time, he being then on his way across the mountains for Rupert's Land. I made known to him my determination to leave the Columbia, and my intention of going to Red River Settlement to see that place. On mentioning Red River, the Governor observed to me, "If you are resolved on leaving the service and going to Red River, I shall have a situation there for you until you have time to look about you." I thanked his Excellency for the offer, and prepared for my journey.

At the entrance of Spokane River, Governor Simpson, chief Factor M'Millan, myself, my son, then eleven years of age, the two Indian boys, Pelly and Garry, together with fifteen men, all embarked on board of two boats, and set out on our way for the Rocky Mountains. The season was early, the weather fine, the grass already long, the trees covered with foliage, and the whole face of nature smiled; every countenance, too, beamed with cheerfulness: I alone was downcast. I had to leave my family behind, who had for years shared with me in the toils and dangers of my travels; this was to me a source of grief and anxiety, although it had been arranged that they were to cross over and join me the following year. On these occasions, the Company afford every facility to families leaving the country; and as it is impossible for women and children to undertake such arduous voyages in the spring of the year—owing to the cold, the high state of the waters, the deep snows in the mountains, and the general hurry and despatch at that season—families in going from one part of the country to another are provided with everything for their comfort and convenience at more favourable seasons. My family reached the mountains in the same autumn, and wintered on the height of land; they thence proceeding early in the spring, joined me in health and good spirits at Red River Colony in the summer of 1826.

But to return to the voyage, from our starting-point to the Rocky Mountains. This has not yet been noticed in our narrative; nor, as far as I know, been described by any person; so that our attention will now be more particularly directed to that part of Columbia as we proceed.

Having started, we passed on to the Kettle Falls, a distance of about 82 miles, which we may call the first stage of our voyage, our course being north-east, and the river full of rapids; the prospects all along were pleasant: woods, plains, hills, and dales, in endless succession. At the Falls, all craft ascending or descending the river have to make a portage, to pass that barrier. These Falls roll over the rocks in various places; they are not, however, more than ten or twelve feet high, and shift from place to place, according to the rising and falling of the water, and the position of the rocks; so that at all stages of the water, the impediments are pretty much the same, for as one place gets better, another gets worse.

This place is a great rendezvous for the natives during the salmon or summer season; but neither the concourse of Indians, nor the quantity of salmon killed at this place, are a tithe of the numbers taken at the Dalles, or at Ama-ketsa's camp in the Snake country.

At this place, the site of a new establishment, to be named "Colville," was marked out, close to the Falls. The situation of Colville has been extolled by many as a delightful spot; there is a small luxuriant vale of some acres in extent, where the fort is to be built, under the brow of a woody height: this is so far pleasant enough, but in every other respect the prospect on all sides is limited. The place is secluded and gloomy; unless the unceasing noise of the Falls in front, and a country skirted on the opposite side of the river with barren and sterile rocks and impenetrable forests in the rear, can compensate for the want of variety in other respects. If so, the place may, indeed, be called delightful; otherwise, there are very few places in this part of the country less attractive, or more wild.

From the Kettle Falls to the lower or Petit Dalles, the second barrier in our journey, a distance of twenty miles, the general course is N.N.W., the river very serpentine, but particularly so for the first six miles, where it forms irregular courses, and yet is smooth and free from rapids. At this place we had to unload, and carried our property over a portage of two hundred yards in length.

As we advanced, a little above the site of Colville, a small stream enters on the west side of the river Sunwhoyellpeatook or White Sheep River. This is the only river that enters the main stream till we reached the Petit Dalles, where the deep and compressed body of water rushes with great velocity through a narrow passage. Here are a number of cylindrical holes, which have been formed by round stones or pebbles, being kept whirling round by the current and the whirlpools, until they have in the course of time made holes of various sizes in the solid rocks; some of them are not larger than a snuff-box, while others are large enough to contain tons of water.

Leaving the Petit Dalles, we proceeded against a strong current until we had reached a distance of sixteen miles, general course north, where the Columbia receives, on the east side, the tributary stream of Flathead River, which we have already traced to its source. At its entrance, where it shoots over a ledge of rocks eight or ten feet high, which bars it across from side to side, it is fifty yards broad, and falls into the main river in one white foaming sheet. This river is sometimes called Pend d'Oreille, sometimes Callispellum; but it is more generally known by the name Flathead River.

Near to this place are several islands of various size; some of them are formed entirely of drift wood, and have enlarged year after year by accumulating quantities which drift down the river; others again are formed of naked rocks which stud the river in various places, interrupting the view and dividing the stream into various channels. As we rounded one of these high rocks one morning, against wind and swell, one of our boats was almost dashed to pieces and nearly upset; our escape was a narrow one, for the rocks stopped our approach, and we only reached the shore by the help of our companion boat. The east side of the river opposite to this is skirted by a range of high land, rendered remarkable by four conspicuous knobs, which show themselves at a distance; here the river is constantly shifting courses.

From the mouth of Flathead River we advanced through a rugged country, for the distance of twenty-four miles, in a northerly direction, without meeting any other impediment than a strong and rapid current. At the end of that distance, as we rounded a low point of woods, on the east side of the river, we came to the Kootanais, commonly called the M'Gillivray River; this latter stream is, at its entrance, double the breadth of the Flathead River, although neither so deep nor so long.

The Kootanais River has its source in the Rocky Mountains: in its westerly and meandering course it passes through a considerable lake, and some time before joining its waters with the Columbia, it shoots over a height of fifteen feet. The entrance of this river is rendered remarkable by having, on the south side, one of those delightful spots which man, in these wilds, is prone to admire; and on the left, the remains of a deserted Indian camp. It is rendered still more remarkable by a dike of round stones, which runs up obliquely against the main stream, on the west side, for more than one hundred yards in length, resembling the foundation of a wall; it is nearly as high as the surface of the water, and is clearly seen at low water. On the opposite or east side is a similar range, of less extent. These are evidently the work of man, and not destitute of ingenuity; we supposed them to be a contrivance for the purpose of catching fish at low water: they are something similar to those used by the Snakes during the salmon season. At the upper end both ranges incline to the centre of the river, where they nearly meet. If the object was to bar the river across, it was certainly a fruitless undertaking. On passing this barrier, the river makes a quick and lengthy bend to the west, and opens to more than its ordinary breadth, for a distance of ten miles.

At the elbow of this bend, on the north side, is a lofty mountain, opposite to which are a large and small island, delightfully situated. The banks are low, diversified with clumps of young poplars, birch, and alder, which give to the surrounding scenery a pleasing appearance. Here the general aspect of the country is agreeable; and we were fortunate enough to find as much level ground as we required to camp on for the night. This brings us to the lower end of the first lake, the appearance of which caused much joy.

In looking back upon the part of the river we

have voyaged, the mind is lost in wonder how such a body of water, free from cascades, could have ever made its way through a country so rocky and mountainous. The river in most places is contracted by the rocky heights on each side, and its low bed makes it appear still more contracted than it really is. The view in most places is limited and gloomy: dark and impenetrable woods generally cover the whole declivity down to the water's edge.

To this part of Columbia, Nature has dealt out her favours with a sparing hand: scarcely anything was to be seen but the river beneath us, and the stern rocks and sombre wood above and around us on every side. Not the least traces of animal have we seen for some days past; equally scarce are the wild fowl; even insects and reptiles seem to have no place here—silence and desolation reign undisturbed. I could say of the few days past what I could not have said before for the last fifteen years—that I had passed a day and slept a night without seeing an Indian, or the trace of any human being: no wonder, then, that we should, after getting clear of so dreary a part of the river, have felt a sensation of relief on beholding the lake expand before us. This brings us to the second stage of our voyage, a distance of fifty miles.

At the entrance of the lake it has the appearance of a large river, with a high and conspicuous knoll overlooking the south-west entrance, which points out its first course—north-west for fifteen miles. During this distance a bold and abrupt range of high lands on each side confine the river between them. Immediately after the banks become low and the beach gravelly, along which are scattered here and there some small cedars and dwarf pines, and in one place a thicket of young firs remarkable for their green and thriving appearance.

At a point on the west side a number of figures of men and animals have been rudely portrayed on the naked rocks with red ochre; and into a large cavity, at a considerable height above high-water mark, a number of arrows have been shot, which remain as a menace left by some distant tribe who had passed there on a warlike expedition. The natives understand these signs, and can tell, on examining the arrows, to which tribe they belong.

On these rocks the high-water mark of former years is indicated by a streak on the stones, and by quantities of drift-wood lodged in the fissures and clefts of the rocks at a distance of more than thirty feet above the present surface of the water. Here the waters are, apparently at least, more productive than the land, for the salmon and other species of fish peculiar to the country sported about in every direction, while the land presented but little to admire. In some parts, however, the trees were of a good size, and not unfrequently spots of rich soil were seen in the valleys.

In these parts we perceived, as we sailed along, a remarkable whiteness on the rocks between the high and low water mark. In other parts, again, we noticed quite a different appearance: some of the rocks showed a reddish, others a greenish hue, not altogether displeasing to the eye. In the distance the general appearance of the country is very pleasing—green, luxuriant, and diversified by thick woods, with open plains, deep valleys, rivulets, and spots of rich pasture.

After the first bend, the course of the lake is due north, and its average breadth about two miles and a half; having a good sailing wind, we soon got through it. At the upper end it contracts to little more than a mile in breadth, and terminates in a course north by east; but its general course throughout is due north. This beautiful sheet of water is forty-two miles long.

Just as we had reached the extreme point of the lake we perceived in the edge of the bushes a thin curl of smoke rising. Taking it for the residence of some living inhabitant, we made for the spot, and there found two Indians squatted before a small fire, but without any lodge, or other shelter than the woods afforded them; one of them was elderly, the other a young man of about twenty years of age, who was suffering severely from a wound in the breast. On inquiring how he came by it, the old man, after some hesitation, related to us the following story:—

"We have been here," said he, "ten days. At first we were a good many persons; but my son," pointing to the wounded man, "had a quarrel with one of his comrades about his wife, after which the man went off, and my son's wife followed him, and we have not seen them since. My son then in a fit of rage for his wife shot himself, as you see, and I am taking care of him." From this it would appear that the inhabitants of the wilderness are subject to fits of jealousy. As soon as the aged father had related his son's misfortune, he began to cry and lament sadly.

They had applied nothing to the wound, but had probed it with a small sharp stick, round the point of which was tied a little of the inner rind of the spruce bark pounded very soft, which kept the wound running,—a painful operation, that had reduced the patient almost to a skeleton. Having nothing else, we gave him a piece of soap to wash the wound, and then left them. The wound was from a gun loaded with shot, which, as far as we could judge, had penetrated almost through the body; but from what I have already seen of wounds amongst Indians, I think it possible he might recover.

At the water's edge we saw and examined a birch-rind canoe of rather singular construction, such as I had never seen in any other part of the country, but used by the natives here; for I saw several of the same make when I passed this place two years ago. Both stem and stern, instead of being raised up in a gentle and regular curve, as is customary elsewhere, lie flat on the surface of the water, and terminate in a point resembling a sturgeon's snout; the upper part is covered, except a space in the middle; its length is 22 feet from point to point, and the whole bottom between these points is a dead level. Such craft must prove exceedingly awkward in rough water; and there is often a heavy swell in these lakes.

We have noticed that the lake terminated in a north-easterly direction, where we, of course, entered the river again. During several miles there were many sand flats, which during high water overflowed, and gave to the place more the appearance of a lake than a river; but the current decides the point in favour of the latter. Near to this place flows on the east side a little river which enters the parent stream through a low woody point, opposite to which, on the west side, is a very conspicuous triangular mountain. The country all round has a most savage and wild appearance. Having proceeded sixteen miles in the same direction as we left the lake, we came to the second, or upper, lake. Here it began to rain, and from rain turned to sleet, ending in a heavy fall of snow; and so very cold was the weather that the men were obliged to have recourse to their mittens and blanket coats: even then, we passed a very cold and disagreeable night.

Just as we had encamped, a stout elderly savage emerged from the rocks behind us. He appeared at first rather surprised, shy, and reserved; but soon recovering his presence of mind, became talkative, and gave us much information respecting the country, beaver and other animals, roads and distances; also some account of himself and the Indians of the place.

"My father," said he, "was a Kootanais chief; but, in consequence of wars with the Blackfeet, who often visited his lands, he and a part of his people emigrated to this country about thirty years ago. I am now chief of that band, and head of all the Indians here. We number about two hundred, and call ourselves Sinatcheggs, the name of the country; and here we have lived ever since. I have been across the land on the west, as far as the Sawthlelum-takut, or Oakanagan Lake, which lies due west from this, and can be travelled on foot in six days. I and several of my people have likewise been to the She-whaps, which lies in a north-west direction from this; but the road leading to the latter place strikes off two days' journey from this, and it takes eight days' travel to accomplish it. We have no horses on our lands, nor is the country suitable for them; we make all our journeys on foot. This part is well stocked with beaver and other kind of furs, and we have in consequence often wished for a trader among us. The lakes abound with sturgeon and other fish; so that we live well, and are at peace with all men."

Here the old man concluded his remarks, and told us that his people were then living about two miles up the river, where they were employed in hunting wild animals and catching fish; that his stumbling upon us was the effect of mere chance, he being at the time in pursuit of a wounded moose deer; but, on seeing the whites, he abandoned the pursuit, and came into our camp. We gave the sachem of the Sinatcheggs an axe, a knife, and some tobacco, and he took his departure highly gratified with his reception.

Notwithstanding the weather was cold and unpleasant, we made an early start, and soon afterwards entered the second lake in a north-westerly course for about ten miles. Everything around was dreary and winter like; and the tops of the highest mountains were covered with snow. The wind proving favourable, we hoisted sail, and proceeded over a clear sheet of deep blue water. On entering the lake, our attention was at once attracted by a number of white objects in the water, resembling at a little distance the appearance of men. On a nearer approach, we found nothing but stumps standing and leaning in every direction, having their lower ends immovably fixed in the sandy bottom.

Two years ago we passed this place in the night, and had great difficulty in keeping our boats from being either upset or broken by them, as they were thickly studded in the channel through which we had to pass. Near the middle of the lake we passed a prominent point of land on the east side, with a high bluff, which we called Cape Rock; opposite to which, on the west, the lake swells out into a considerable bay, where the course inclines more to the north. On the same side is a high peak, treeless on the top, and capped with snow: this peak marks the broadest part of the lake. Looking northward from this point, the lake appears very beautiful; but the view is interrupted by a lofty mountain, which at a distance appears to bar the channel across, and terminates the lake. We had no sooner arrived there than on looking back we saw plainly the lofty top of the triangular mountain passed at the upper end of the first lake.

This body of water is in general broader, and has a much finer appearance, than the other lake; but the shores are more rocky. Its length is about thirty-three miles, its breadth three miles, and it lies in the direction of north and south. As we sailed along, we perceived several small rivers or creeks enter it on either side; but none of them of a size to merit particular attention. The face of the country generally is varied, broken, and mountainous. On one occasion our attention was directed to a small Indian hut close by the water, and a child about four or five years of age, endeavouring to make its escape into the woods, by climbing up the steep bank. As we approached the place, it began to scream out, and tried again to get up, but failed; at last, however, it made a successful effort, got up, and was out of sight in the bushes, before we could land. On jumping ashore, as we were anxious to see some more of the Indians, we speedily followed after, got hold of the little fellow and brought him back to the hut. All this time we saw nobody else; but had no sooner showed ourselves to be friends, and pacified the little urchin by acts of kindness, than an elderly woman made her appearance out of a cleft of the rocks, and after her two little girls crept out from the same hiding-place. We spoke to them, and gave them a few trifles; when the old woman ran off and brought us some roots and berries, which she laid down before us; we then shook each of them by the hand and parted good friends.

The natives we have seen in these parts are few and far between, and in their habits resemble wild animals; they seem to have no recognised camp like other Indians. If the good old chief told us the truth, that he was their pastor, or head, he has a very scattered and wretched flock.

From the lower end of the first lake, all along to this place, the country presents a varied aspect, and we not unfrequently saw delightful spots that will, at some future day, prove the comfortable abode of civilised man.

In taking leave of the lakes, we entered the river in the usual course of north-west. At the end of two miles we passed, on the east side, a cataract, which shot over a precipice some thirty feet high; the water was clear as crystal and as cold as ice. Near to the same spot is a fine thicket of stately cedars, which we called Cedar Grove. Five miles from Cataract Creek, we passed an island which, from having started several deer on it, we named Deer Island; it is more than half a mile in length, and formed entirely of driftwood, as appears from the outer edges of it: the force of the current has compressed the wood so closely and solidly together, that it seems to have been laid in tiers, as by the hands of man. The main body of the island has become one solid mass of decayed vegetation; out of which are seen growing pines, poplars, and a variety of trees, some of them measuring two feet in diameter. Yet much of the original wood of which the island was at first composed is still solid, and in a good state of preservation, although, perhaps, it had lain imbedded there for more than a hundred years, and the surface or sward, formed on the top from year to year, has increased the solid earth to the thickness of several feet. In one or two places we saw islands of this description beginning to be formed.

During the voyage we have generally omitted

to notice the numerous islands scattered throughout the river, they presenting but little variety, for except those that are purely rocky, they are chiefly composed of drift wood. The immense quantities which float down the river yearly, either with the ice in the spring or during high water, are often obstructed in the channel by sunken rocks; or the wood itself getting entangled, compressed, and forced together by the current and ice, or fixed in the sandy bottom, forms a nucleus, which keeps accumulating until an island is formed.

In many places, notwithstanding the mountainous aspect of the country and rocky shores, the current for short distances is smooth, and free from rapids: from Deer Island to Otter Creek, a distance of eight miles, this is the general character of the river. But from the latter to a place called the Upper Little Narrows, there is a very dangerous place of more than a mile in length, lying in the direction of east and west, a distance of fifteen miles: the river there is full of rapids. Between Deer Island and the Narrows are to be seen numerous sandy flats, remarkable for the number and variety of shining particles—substances resembling different kinds of ores, lying scattered almost everywhere along the beach, and among the sand and rocks.*

In doubling one of many rapid points which almost everywhere arrest the progress of the

---

* A kind of talc common in that part of America.

voyageur, the body of water was so strong and rapid, that we failed with the paddle, setting-pole, and line four times, in our attempts to ascend, and only got up the fifth; we therefore named the place Point Try-it-again. At the head of this rapid we had to cross the river, where the force of the water was so great, that our boats were whirled round on the surface by cross currents, so that they were in the utmost danger of being swallowed up: one of the shocks was so sudden that all hands were unseated.

Within the distance of seven miles we passed eighteen strong rapids, crossed and recrossed the river (to avoid bad places) one hundred and twelve times, and passed in that distance sixteen cataracts, which poured their tribute into the parent stream.

Few places can present a more gloomy or perilous prospect to the voyageur than the Little Narrows; for about a mile the view is almost completely shut up between mountains and rocks; and in getting our boats through, they were tossed from side to side, leaving but little hope at times of their ever getting up without accident. At the head of this intricate passage, which we fortunately got over in safety, the river forms endless windings, for a distance of about ten miles; when it enters, on the east side, a considerable stream, which we have named Beaver Creek, from the ravages of that industrious animal seen about its banks. Here also the tracks of deer and elk were seen, and some wild ducks and geese.

From the Narrows to Beaver River the general aspect is diversified, from the hilly to the rocky and mountainous, the channel being more or less rapid, and the stones along the beach almost everywhere incrusted with a metallic substance resembling black-lead, which gives them a smooth and glossy appearance. Here also the shining particles we noticed some time ago have become more and more abundant; when the sun shines, they appear like bits of tinsel lace, and are so dazzling as to affect the eyes.

At the distance of twelve miles, in the usual course of north-west from Beaver Creek, there is a remarkable height on the east side of the river; it is partly covered with snow, and partly with numerous towering rocks, broken fragments, peaks, and serrated ranges, resembling the turrets, domes, spires, and steeples of a city in ruins. What stamps the impression of reality still more forcibly is the cloud of mist that floats above this imaginary city; and the longer we looked at it, the stronger was the illusion, so deceptive are objects seen with the naked eye at a distance.

Twenty-two miles beyond the City of Rocks, a fine river enters the Columbia, on the same side as Beaver Creek. The largest we have met with since passing the Kootanais River, I have named M'Kenzie's River, after my companion and fellow traveller of former years, M'Kenzie of Mayville. At its entrance, and on its banks, were numerous tracks of the beaver, moose deer, and other animals; fresh bear tracks were also numerous.

At a short distance above the M'Kenzie River commence the Grand Rapids, or Dalles des Morts. These Dalles are about two miles in length from end to end, in the direction of south-east and north-west; and at the head of them is an abrupt bend, forming the most dangerous part. Here the channel, which is scarcely forty yards broad, presents a succession of white breakers, and a portage of one hundred and fifty yards must be made, where everything but the boats has to be carried. At the bend or narrowest part of this intricate passage, the river appears to have forced a passage for itself through the solid rock; but the huge sides of the yawning chasm seem to threaten to resume their former position by closing up the gap.

In the portage, the road by land is no less difficult, and but little less dangerous, than the passage by water; yet the adroit voyageur disregarding all dangers, overcomes all difficulties. After three hours' labour we landed the boats safely at the upper end, paying but little attention to the objects around us. Here many have closed their career, and found a watery grave: here is to be seen a cross, there a solitary grave, to tell their sad but silent tale. Yet for all these warnings the boatmen heedlessly push on, as if nothing had ever happened to those who had gone before them!

A prospect more wild and dangerous than the Grand Rapids we have seldom seen: at the upper end is the spot where, in 1816, four of our men perished. On this melancholy place stands, near to the water's edge, a wide-spreading pine-tree, occupying the place of the weeping willow; and close by it is a lofty square rock, on which we inscribed their names. We then, in silence, turned our backs on the Dalles des Morts, a distance from the Lakes of seventy-five miles: this forms the fourth stage of our journey.

From the upper end of the Grand Rapids, our course leads due north; and here, a little after starting, we backed our paddles, and stood still for some minutes, admiring a striking natural curiosity on the east side. The water of a cataract creek, after shooting over the brink of a bold precipice, falls in a white sheet on to a broad flat rock, smooth as glass, which forms the first step; then upon a second, some ten feet lower down; and lastly on a third, somewhat lower; it then enters a subterraneous vault, formed at the mouth like a funnel, and after passing through this funnel it again issues forth, with the noise of distant thunder; after falling over another step, it meets the front of a bold rock, which repulses back the water with such violence as to keep it whirling round in a large basin; opposite to this rises the wing of a shelving cliff, which overhangs the basin, and forces back the rising spray, refracting in the sunshine all the colours of the rainbow. The creek then enters the Columbia.

As we rounded Point Curiosity, a name we gave to this place, we shot at a black bear, which although badly wounded, got into the woods, and we had no time to follow it. Soon afterwards we saw some deer, and fired several shots at them, two of them being killed on the spot. In these parts, the constant fogs create so much humidity that the air is always extremely damp; even in fine weather sportsmen must prime their guns anew, or they will have but a poor chance of killing much game: percussion guns would answer best in this climate. As we advance, the river assumes a smoother surface, and the country, for a short distance, assumes a more pleasing aspect.

Four miles from the Grand Rapids we passed a cluster of rocky fragments, which obtained the name of Castle Rock, from its singular appearance. Near this place we picked up several pieces of lead and iron ores; the stones lying along the beach were also variegated, and no less singular for their whimsical shapes and colours, than remarkable for a peculiar roughness of surface, resembling the rust of old iron or coarse sand-paper; others were coated with a crust like black-lead, nor have the shining particles among the sand and rocks diminished.

All the way from M'Kenzie's River up to Castle Rock the country is remarkable for its gloomy aspect, and the banks along the river for the number and variety of spangled or shining substances, which everywhere attract attention.

And here, while surrounded with so many novelties, one of our men, rather a green hand from Canada, was so much delighted with the spangled substances, that he fancied himself in one of the gold-mines of Peru; for he gathered together and bagged nearly a bushel of these shining treasures, saying to his companions that he would enrich himself by selling them in his own country for gold and silver.

At the distance of eight miles from Castle Rock is Egg-shell Island; this must be a great resort for wild fowl in the summer season, as we found great numbers of egg-shells scattered about the place. On the east side, and about nine miles from Egg-shell Island, a fine stream enters the river; the first we have met with above the Grand Rapids worth notice. Arriving at its entrance, we perceived some elk crossing it, when I and one of the men set off in pursuit of them; but we had to return, after a fruitless chase of more than an hour, tired and unsuccessful, with our clothes literally torn to rags. On our arrival, some of the voyageurs, in a jocular mood, called out, "We must name the river after Mr. Ross," and the name remained. Ross's River is deeper, but not so broad as M'Kenzie's, and it is a fine navigable stream for canoes.

On the same side as Ross's River, we came to a

place resembling an amphitheatre, with galleries, boxes, and pit, as if cut out of the cliff by the hand of man. This huge structure hangs rather loosely and suspiciously over the side of the river, and appears so awkwardly supported, that we were rather alarmed to pass near it: this strange-looking place, which we named the Circus, is about twelve miles beyond Ross's River. Near to it were three Indian birch-rind canoes laying on the beach, turned upside down; but not a human being was to be seen about the place. Not far from the Circus, we passed Rapid Crôche, so called from its very crooked and serpentine appearance; and near to it Diamond Creek, a small stream remarkable for the brilliant particles along its banks. Though then small, yet if we may judge from the size of the channel, a great and irresistible body of water must discharge itself there at some season of the year; for its banks, which are low and flat, are covered with large stones, trees, and drift wood, which must have been hurled down by the force of the current.

Eight miles beyond the Circus, we passed a group of little islands, where beaver ravages were to be seen; from which circumstance we named them Beaver Islands. Here we saw some geese, and a few diving ducks, commonly called water-hens; we likewise saw two red squirrels, and some small butterflies, the first of the kind we had noticed during the voyage. At this place the mosquitoes were very troublesome, notwithstanding the weather was cold enough for blankets. A little distance from Beaver Islands, a very pleasantly situated small river forms the main stream on the west side; I named it M'Millan's River, as a tribute of friendship for James M'Millan, Esquire, formerly of Columbia. Floating down this river, we noticed numbers of black flies, large and small, called the snow-fly; we skimmed them off the surface of the water with our hands, and many of them still showed symptoms of life. Such is the dampness of the climate here, that the smaller insects have neither activity nor vigour to save themselves by flight, except in the sunshine. In fact, the state of the weather in these parts has a peculiar influence over the whole face of nature: in a dark day, everything appears in the most dismal light, whereas if the sun happens to shine, the rudest of Nature's works seem to smile and produce a strikingly agreeable effect.

From M'Millan's River, a distance of eight miles, we came to a considerable height, from which we had a rather pleasing prospect. This place I called Belle Vue Point. Here we had the first view of the Rocky Mountains, lying northeast, distant about ten miles; and rocky, indeed, is their appearance. Between the river we have just named and Belle Vue Point the surrounding aspect was strikingly wild and romantic; an endless variety of towering heights, rugged peaks, and snow-capped mountains everywhere studded the broken and barren surface.

After passing Belle Vue Point, the country was more agreeable, and the river also; but this improvement was but of short duration, for we had only time to pass a point or two when the aspect became gloomy, and the rapids and bad steps as frequent as ever. As we advanced and viewed the river ahead of us, it appeared to contract like the tube of a funnel, and lose itself in the mountains; we, however, no sooner advanced to where it seemed to terminate, than the mountains receded, a passage presented itself, and we again beheld the channel wide and navigable as ever, inviting us to advance.

Again and again were we encouraged, until we reached Crystal Creek, some two miles from Belle Vue Point; here, however, the mountains closed in so near to each other as to confine the view to the rocky heights on each side and the sky above us: and here, indeed, the abrupt turnings of the river seemed to preclude all hopes of any further progress; yet we persevered, and our efforts were crowned with success. For two days past we had been following these short windings, and doubtful points, where we could scarcely at any time see the course of the river for half a mile.

At last we reached a small opening, and were relieved, inasmuch as we could see about us. Notwithstanding the intricate windings, and mountainous state of the country, the river is by no means bad; nor are the rapids or other difficult passages to be compared, either for danger or difficulty, to many places we had already passed. We had no sooner passed this opening than the mountains closed in again upon the river, where the rapids and difficult places became more and more frequent; but the active and adroit voyageurs seemed to disregard all obstacles, and with paddle and pole alternately, set all difficulties at defiance.

The Canadians are clever voyageurs; in the worst places, when the steersman calls out briskly, "Tout à la fois: tout ensemble," giving a flourish or two with his paddle, the effort they make is seldom unsuccessful, and all generally ends well. At the distance of six miles from Crystal Creek, we arrived at the entrance of Canoe River, coming in from the north-west, and about forty yards broad at its mouth: this is the river I visited from the She-whaps, across land, in September, 1816.

Here the main river veers gradually round, from north-east to south-east, and marks the northernmost point of Columbia River. A little beyond Canoe River a rapid little stream enters on the east or mountain side, coming direct from the height of land, which we shall have occasion to mention more particularly hereafter: this stream I have named Portage River. Opposite to it, the Columbia spreads out, covering, during high water, a space of four hundred yards in breadth; but at low water it divides into three separate channels each about fifty yards broad: the eastern channel is the best, but all of them are shoal, and flow rapidly over a rocky bottom; here, however, the south channel spreads out, and finds its way among the woods, as the bank there is low. From Portage River the Columbia, in a south-east direction, skirts the base of the mountains all along to its source, a distance from our present position, following the circuitous course of the river, of one hundred and eighty miles, and it is navigable for boats more than half the way.

According to the rough calculations we have been able to make, this branch of the Columbia, in all its windings, from the Great Forks near Fort Nez Percés up to its source, may be considered 820 miles long. It offers a wide field to the mineralogist, and unlimited employment to the lover of natural history. Portage River, which is about thirty yards wide, enters the Columbia at right angles, and forms Portage Point. Here we landed, secured our boats, and prepared for our journey across the mountains; which makes the fifth stage of our route, and is a distance of sixty-eight miles from the Grand Rapids. And this terminates our voyage on the waters of the Columbia.

CHAPTER XV.

Portage Point—Wild scenery—Forbidding prospect—The five tribes—Begin the portage—The walking-stick Journal—Hard day's work—Luxuries of the evening camp—Road described—Leave Portage River—Scenery—Portage Valley—Climbing the Grand Côte—Size of the timber—Encampment—Night scene—Punch-bowl Lake—Sister Creeks—Farewell to Columbia—Avalanches—Devastation—Giant of the rocks—Horses arrive—Road obstructions—The Hole—Athabasca—Length of portage—East side scenery—First establishment—North-westers and bark canoes—Jasper's house——Lapensie's grave—Solitary travelling—Fort Assiniboine—Exchange horses for canoes—The new road—Sturgeon River—The party described—Garments—Arrive at Fort Edmonton—Indians—Trade—A ball—Offensive dogs—Saskatchewan boats—Charming scenery—Fort Carlton—Hostile Indians—Agriculture—The swampy country—Crees—Fort Cumberland—Sturgeon—Trade—Gardens—The sun-dial—Domestic cattle—Lake Bourbon—Arctic land expedition—Franklin and Richardson—The country of frogs and mosquitoes—Grand rapid—Miskagoes—Winipeg—Mossy Point—Arrive at Norway house—Migratory habits of the warlike tribes of the plains—Views of the introduction of agriculture—Mr. Leith's bequest.

WITH the last chapter we closed our remarks on the water navigation of the Columbia, as far as Portage Point, or as it has since been named Boat-Encampment; the spot from whence I turned back two years ago. But before leaving this stage of our journey, I will make a few observations on this interesting place.

Here the spectator has on one side a picturesque view of most diversified scenery. The only opening that anywhere presents itself is on the south-west side; and looking in that direction, we saw the main stream before us; the upper branch flowing from the south-east on one hand, and Canoe River and a parting glance of the descending Columbia visible on the other. Turning round to the east, the view is abruptly checked by the mountains; not in a continuous range, but heights rising one above another, almost everywhere shrouded in a dark haze, which renders a passage over them extremely doubtful. Yet through this apparently inaccessible barrier the traveller has to make his way.

We shall now glance at the country intervening between Portage Point, the northernmost part of the great north branch, and Cape Clear Weather, the southernmost point of the still greater south branch of Columbia; where both rivers verge in the mountains, at a distance of some seven hundred miles apart. The figure of the country thus embraced represents a triangle, the base of which skirts the Rocky Mountains, and terminates in a point at the Great Forks, near Fort Nez Percés. The northern section is well wooded and watered; but the character of the southern quarter is arid and mountainous: yet, as a whole, it is a delightful country in summer.

Considering its extent, climate, animals of the chase, horses, and scalps, all these temptations hold out enticing prospects of booty to the marauding brigands east of the mountains; who, in consequence, visit it too frequently. It is the great theatre of war, and the land for horse thieves; which may account for the scanty population. If we leave out of the account casual visits of the War-are-ree-kas, the few mountain Snakes on the south, and the still fewer Sinatcheggs on the north, there are only five petty tribes resident in all this quarter: namely, the Kootanais and Selish, or Flatheads, at the foot of the mountains, and the Pointed-hearts, Pend d'Oreilles, and Spokanes lower down; the whole not mustering more than 1850 souls.

As we ascended the river, we saw but few traces of animals; but when we happened to go any distance into the woods, or from the river, fresh tracks were so frequent as to cross each other in all directions, particularly of the beaver.

Return we now for a moment to Portage Point, where we arrived at nine o'clock in the morning: such was our despatch, that we had no sooner concluded our voyage by water, and laid up our boats on land, than, in the space of an hour, our arrangements for the arduous task of crossing the mountains were completed.

With a load of ninety pounds' weight on each man's back, and each carrying his gun and blanket, we set out in a string one after another, on a narrow footpath across a low quagmire, overflowed in many places with a foot or more of snow-water. After proceeding for some distance, we crossed a low and wet woody point; then travelling nine miles in an easterly course, we again fell on Portage River; on the wet and stony beach of which we spread our blankets, and passed the night. Where Portage River enters the Columbia, the current for some distance is slack, but at our encampment it flowed very swiftly.

After passing a cold night, owing to the wet state of everything around us, we commenced our journey at daybreak. A plunge or two in the cold water was our morning dram, which we had to repeat more frequently than we wished: in short, our whole day was occupied in crossing and recrossing this impetuous torrent.

When the current proves too strong or the water too deep for one person to attempt it alone, the whole join hands together, forming a chain, and thus cross in an oblique line, to break the strength of the current; the tallest always leading the van. By their united efforts, when a light person is swept off his feet, which not unfrequently happens, the party drag him along; and the first who reaches the shore always lays hold of the branches of some friendly tree or bush that may be in the way; the second does the same, and so on till all get out of the water. But often they are no sooner out than in again;

and perhaps several traverses will have to be made within the space of a hundred yards, and sometimes within a few yards of each other; just as the rocks, or other impediments bar the way. After crossing several times, I regretted that I had not begun sooner to count the number; but before night, I had sixty-two traverses marked on my walking-stick, which served as my journal throughout the day.

When not among ice and snow, or in the water, we had to walk on a stony beach, or on gravelly flats, being constantly in and out of the water: many had got their feet blistered, which was extremely painful. The cold made us advance at a quick pace, to keep ourselves warm; and despatch was the order of the day. The Governor himself, generally at the head, made the first plunge into the water, and was not the last to get out. His smile encouraged others, and his example checked murmuring. At a crossing-place there was seldom a moment's hesitation; all plunged in, and had to get out as they could. And we had to be lightly clad, so as to drag less water. Our general course to-day was north-east, but we had at times to follow every point of the compass, and might have travelled altogether twenty miles, although in a direct line we scarcely advanced eight. The ascent appeared to be gradual, yet the contrary was indicated by the rapidity of the current. After a day of excessive fatigue, we halted at dusk, cooked our suppers, dried our clothes, smoked our pipes, then, each spreading his blanket, we laid ourselves down to rest; and, perhaps, of all rest, that enjoyed on the voyage, after a hard day's labour, is the sweetest.

To give a correct idea of this part of our journey, let the reader picture in his own mind a dark, narrow defile, skirted on one side by a chain of inaccessible mountains, rising to a great height, covered with snow, and slippery with ice from their tops down to the water's edge. And on the other side, a beach comparatively low, but studded in an irregular manner with standing and fallen trees, rocks, and ice, and full of drift-wood; over which the torrent everywhere rushes with such irresistible impetuosity, that very few would dare to adventure themselves in the stream. Let him again imagine a rapid river descending from some great height, filling up the whole channel between the rocky precipices on the south and the no less dangerous barrier on the north. And lastly, let him suppose that we were obliged to make our way on foot against such a torrent, by crossing and recrossing it in all its turns and windings from morning till night, up to the middle in water,—and he will understand that we have not exaggerated the difficulties to be overcome in crossing the Rocky Mountains.

On the third morning, at daylight, we were again on our journey; but found our legs stiff and our feet sore after the fatigues of yesterday. The cold water had benumbed every joint and limb; it was with the utmost reluctance we could reconcile ourselves to plunge into this cold and impetuous torrent again, on getting up in the morning. But we had no choice; so we continued our route, although crossing far less frequently than before, until we had travelled three miles. At this place the mountains recede on one side, and on the other the country becomes lower, forming a valley, with a varied and beachy surface, but during the summer becomes an inland lake; over this valley we journeyed for about two miles further, when we arrived at the foot of the principal hill, commonly called the Grande Côte. Here we leave the river to the left, our road leading to the right.

At this place Portage River is scarcely twenty yards broad; but the width of the channel and the traces of ravages left by the water among the woods and rocks show that a powerful and impetuous body of water descends here at some season of the year; yet the general aspect is altogether improved, and the country more open on the west, and more pleasing than many places we had passed further down.

At nine o'clock in the morning we commenced the ascent of the Grande Côte, and continued to ascend in a thousand sinuous windings till five o'clock in the afternoon; we then found ourselves on the top of it, a distance of about three miles in length, but scarcely a mile and a quarter in a straight line. At first the ascent was gradual, but it increased in difficulty as we advanced; and this was the more keenly felt as we became fatigued and tired of the task. In some places the ascent was so precipitous, and the short and intricate turnings so steep, that we had to get up them by clinging to the branches that stood in our way, and we not unfrequently had recourse to our hands and knees; when this failed we had to be assisted by each other, dragging first the man, and then his load up, before we got to the summit. None but a voyageur or Indian can comprehend how men with heavy loads could accomplish such a task. And much greater would his surprise be if told that at certain seasons, when the snows are off the ground, loaded horses ascend and descend this route as far as Portage Point, and that few accidents ever occur.

But although we were now on the top of the Grande Côte, or Bell Hill, let not the reader imagine that we had reached the highest part of the Rocky Mountains; for we saw heights towering above heights, until their distant summits were lost in the clouds. I therefore considered that the place we now stood on was about half way from the base of the Grande Côte to the top of the highest rock we saw above us. The forest scenery, even at this height, imparted variety, and relieved the eye from the dull monotony of rocks and glaciers which everywhere surrounded us. At the base the woods were thick, and the trees measured from two to two-and-a-half feet in diameter; and all along the ascent the trees, although not so numerous as below, were yet about the same size; but on the top I found only a few that measured more than a foot in diameter.

On the summit of the Grande Côte we found the snow eight feet deep, and there we encamped for the night. When travelling over snow, it is always customary for travellers to clear a spot for their encampment; but the men were so worn out after their day's labour, that a little indulgence was shown them on the present occasion. After throwing the loads off their backs, instead of setting them to clear away the snow and pitch the tents as usual, they were ordered to lay a tier of long green wood on the surface of the snow; upon which, after being covered over with wet faggots and brushwood, a blazing fire was kindled and we prepared for rest. Travellers in severe weather, in these parts, generally sleep with their feet towards the fire; it was so with us, as no regular encampment was made. Each rolling himself up in his blanket, lay down on the surface of the snow, with his feet to the centre, forming a circle round the cheering fire; every one stuck his shoes and socks on a forked stick to dry, in order to be ready for an early start. This being done, sleep soon sealed up our eyes.

We were not, however, long permitted to enjoy a bed of snow in peace; for hardly had we slept, when one poor fellow, who had placed his feet in rather doubtful proximity to the fire, was awakened by feeling it approach too near his toes. Thus warned, he started up, exclaiming, "Le feu! le feu!" In a moment we were roused; but only to witness a scene of confusion, mingled with jests and shouts of laughter. It appeared that the fire had sunk down a considerable way, owing to the melting of the snow under it, and thus formed a miniature crater, over which feet and blankets, as well as shoes and socks, had experienced a too warm temperature. On jumping up, some, not aware of their position, slid down, with an easy descent, into the fiery gulph; but, fortunately, the melted snow which they carried down with them, and the activity of their comrades, who hastily dragged them up, prevented anything more serious than a fright. Some, however, were slightly burned; but none received any serious injury. The best part of the joke was, that some one threw the poor fellow's bag of stones, which he had collected along the way, and on which he set so much value, into the fiery pit, and the distracted man had a hard scramble to rescue his fossil treasures. Before we had got all our odds and ends together, it was broad daylight; we, therefore, set out on our journey, promising never again to encamp on the surface of the snow.

Leaving now the Grande Côte, we advanced on the morning crust at a quick pace, through a broad level valley, thickly wooded with dwarf pines, for about six miles in an easterly direction, when we reached what is called the great height of land. At this place is a small circular basin of water, twenty yards in diameter, dignified with the name of a lake, out of which flow two small creeks. The one on the west side discharges itself into Portage River; that on the east joins the Athabasca River at a place called the Hole. This elevated pond is further dignified with the name of the "Committee's Punch Bowl," in honour of which his Excellency treated us to a bottle of wine, as we had neither time nor convenience to make a bowl of punch; although a glass of it would have been very acceptable. It is a tribute always paid to this place when a nabob of the fur trade passes by.

Here I made a halt, turned round, and took a last farewell of Columbia, with all its tributaries; and in doing so, I felt for the first time that I was in one country, and my family in another. Notwithstanding the many anxious days and hairbreadth escapes I had undergone on the west side of the Rocky Mountains and on the shores of the Pacific during a period of fifteen years, I felt at this moment a pang of regret at leaving it.

From Punch Bowl Lake we hastened on through the same valley till we reached, at the end of fourteen miles, the Grand Batteur; there we put up for the night, not forgetting, however, to clear off the snow, and place our fire on the solid earth. The road over which we journeyed to-day was not bad; but, as an instance of its desolation, one solitary mountain hawk was all we saw of the feathered tribes. On our way hither, our attention was drawn to various parts, in consequence of occasionally hearing a loud and rumbling noise, not unlike that of distant thunder, or rather volcanic irruptions; and on looking in the direction from whence the noise proceeded, we always saw a dense volume of smoke rising up like a cloud of dust in dry weather. This, after some time, we discovered to be the sliding down of immense bodies of snow and ice from the overhanging cliffs and precipices of the mountains, sweeping along in their descent, rocks, stones, trees, and everything that happened to lie in the way.

One of those avalanches had fallen on the right hand of the valley through which we were journeying. It lay spread over a space of 540 paces, and extended far out into the valley. The height from which this sheet fell could not be less than 1500 feet. We, therefore, did not consider it safe to be travelling under such awful heights, nor did we select any such places for our encampments at night.

Not far from this place is a very singular rock, placed on the shoulder of another. This huge and conspicuous block we named the Giant of the Rocks. The bold and rugged features of the prospect here defy all description.

With the morning dawn we left the Grand Batteur, passing a chilly and disagreeable night, from the mountains of snow around us: the snow had, however, diminished here to about twenty inches. We had only advanced a few miles, when we had the good fortune to meet, at Campment d'Original, two of the Company's men from the nearest trading post, on the east side of the mountains, with a band of light horses for our service. This meeting, by men tired and worn out with fatigue, was a source of much joy; and we were on the look out for them, for horses are always provided, at both spring and fall, for the purposes of transport, and to assist the foot-passengers and families.

On meeting the horses, we breakfasted, mounted, and continued our journey. Here the men were relieved of their burdens, so that all went on cheerfully until we reached the end of the portage, at a place called the Hole, from the depth of the water at the edge of the bank, the Athabasca being unfathomable there. Course east; distance twenty-two miles.

Punch Bowl Creek, swelled at last to the size of a moderate river, runs along through the same valley, parallel to the road we travelled, and discharges itself into the Athabasca at the Hole, as we have already noticed, where the broad side of that river abruptly met us on emerging from the woods. It lies in the direction of north and south, and flows in the latter course. It is a fine stream, sixty-five yards broad, and skirts close along the base of the mountains. Our road thus far was much obstructed by fallen timber, through which the fire had passed, lying pell mell on the ground, imbedded in ice and snow; to get over or through which was just as much as our horses could do. Crossing the Athabasca at the Hole, we journeyed along the east bank for some miles, until it unites at right angles with another river of nearly equal size, which enters on the east side. This stream we crossed also, and encamped, after a hard day's travel, at the Grande Traverse.

We had now left the Athabasca portage behind us, and got clear of the mountains, and computed the distance from Portage Point to the Hole at eighty-five miles. On reaching the Hole, the mountains abruptly terminate in a uniform range, and present a bold and stupendous wall of great elevation. On the east side, the country at once opens into a wide and boundless prairie—the land of buffalo, and the hunter's paradise. Of the different passes and portages through these mountains, with which I am acquainted, the Athabasca, which we have just crossed, is perhaps the longest, as well as the most gloomy and difficult; owing chiefly to the water in Portage Valley. The Kootanais Pass, the route by Hell's Gates, or the Valley of Troubles, are all less tedious, if taken in the proper season, and the obstacles they present are more easily overcome than those of the Athabasca; yet the Athabasca itself can be travelled from one end to the other on horseback, with the exception of one or two steps in the Grande Côte.

On decamping from the Grande Traverse, we

pursued our journey for ten miles in a northerly direction, until we reached the first post, called the Rocky Mountain House, where we left our horses, and prepared for taking the paddle. On approaching this establishment, situated under the brow of the mountain ridge, we had anticipated a gloomy place; but the very reverse was the case. We advanced, from the water's edge, up an inclined plane, some two or three hundred yards in length, smooth as a bowling-green, and skirted on each side by regular rows of trees and shrubs, the whole presenting the appearance of an avenue leading to some great man's castle, which had a very pleasing effect. Here, however, we found no lordly dwellings, but a neat little group of wood huts suited to the climate of the country, rendered comfortable and filled with cheerful and happy inmates; and what gave to the place a cheering aspect was the young grass, forming a pleasing contrast to the snow-clad heights around.

Here my old friend Joseph Felix Larocque, Esq., an old north-wester, and formerly of Columbia, was in charge; and with his usual kindness, treated us to a dish of very fine titameg, or white fish, the first of the kind I had ever seen. The white fish here is considered, in point of quality, in the same light as salmon on the Columbia, the finest fish in the country; and many an argument takes place whenever parties east and west of the mountains meet, as to which is the best. The Columbians, as a matter of course, argue in favour of the semetleck, or salmon; while the adverse party advocate as strongly the titameg, or white fish. Delicious, however, as we found the titameg, there was nothing either in the taste or flavour to induce me to alter the opinion I had formed. I give the preference to the good old salmon, as the king of all the piscatory tribes on either side of the mountains.

After two hours' delay we said good-bye to Mr. Larocque, and, embarking in two canoes, took the current down the Athabasca. Wherever there is a north-wester in this country, the birch-rind canoe is sure to be found. Although boats would have been far more safe and suitable for our purpose, yet we had to embark in those fragile shells to shoot a dangerous stream. After proceeding for some distance, we put ashore at the first lake, merely an enlargement of the river; but here everything is dignified with the name of lake.

The country lying east of the mountains being generally better known than that on the west, we shall be less minute in our details, and touch as seldom as possible on things already known.

Starting at an early hour, we passed through the first lake, and found at the end of the second, another establishment, named "Jasper's House," still smaller, and of less importance than the first, so called in honour of the first adventurer who established it; but now in charge of a man by the name of Klyne, a jolly old fellow, with a large family. Attached to this petty post are only a few indolent freemen: not an Indian did we see about the place. Here we breakfasted, spent half an hour, and again took the current.

From Jasper's House the river widens and becomes larger; the current strong, and rapids frequent. Their appearance admonished us to proceed with great caution; yet with all our care, we broke one of our canoes, and before we could get to shore our bark was half filled. Ten minutes' delay, and we were again on the water; but had not gone far before a second disaster sent us ashore. At this place a wooden cross was stuck up in the edge of the woods, and on examining it, I found it marked the grave of one of the old Tonquin adventurers noticed in the first part of our narrative. On it was cut, in still legible characters, "Oliviè Lapensie, from Lachine, drowned here in May, 1814."

Leaving Lapensie's Island, the thick woods on our left closed in to the beach, and cast a dismal gloom on the place; but on the right, the country presented a more open and level aspect. If we except the few individuals seen at the establishments, not another living being did we see, either civilised or savage, till we had reached the Company's third establishment, called Fort Assiniboine; a petty post erected on the north bank of the river, and so completely embosomed in the woods, that we did not catch a glimpse of it until we were among huts, and surrounded by howling dogs and screeching children. At this sylvan retreat, there were but three rude houses. Two white men, and six half-breeds, were all the men we saw about the place, and there was not a picket or palisade to guard them from either savage or bear; which said a great deal for the peaceable state of the country. This mean abode was dignified with the name of fort; and with the presence of a chief factor. It is right to observe, however, that Fort Assiniboine was but a new place, in process of building.

Here we exchanged our canoes for horses, and leaving the Athabasca, we prepared to travel by land, intending to strike across the country in a southeasterly direction for the Saskatchewan River; after an hour and a half's delay, we shook hands with McKintosh, crossed the river, mounted our horses, and set off on what was called the new road. In company with us, were some of the half-breed stragglers of the place, who found it convenient to join us in our march; and a strange and grotesque medley our cavalcade formed. Our new companions called themselves half-breeds, but in my opinion there was not a drop of white blood in their veins.

The road formerly in use between the Athabasca and Saskatchewan River, in this place, being always very wet and boggy at this season, it was judged advisable to try some new path, and on it we set out; but after some days' travel, we had little reason to congratulate ourselves, for the new road proved decidedly worse than the old. The wet weather, together with sleet and snow, added to our difficulties.

At any dry season of the year, however, when the snow is off the ground, the road we took, with the exception of the fallen timber, would be preferable to the old pass. In addition, however, to other difficulties, three deep and miry rivers cross both the old and new path; where, instead of our horses carrying us, we had to drag them, as we had perhaps more interest in saving them than they in saving us. So soft and miry were the bottoms and banks of those watercourses, particularly the last one, called Sturgeon River, that we had to dismount and get over it with our horses following us. Afterwards our way lay over a high level plain, where we made a halt to refresh our worn-out animals, and brush up ourselves a little before arriving among strangers.

While marching, our cavalcade resembled an Indian scouting party more than anything else; for except at camping time, the party was never together. During the day, every one rambled about as his fancy led him, either in quest of game or pleasure. On all such excursions the Indians are to be seen occasionally, gazing on the top of some eminence or conspicuous place, like spies on the look out; and they seldom approach the camp otherwise than at full speed, as if bringing some pressing intelligence, and generally amuse themselves with a few notes of some barbarous song. Thus the hardy veterans perambulate the most gloomy wildernesses and are always at home, and from day to day and from meal to meal, depend upon chance for their meat, drink, and clothing; yet they are, in their condition, the happiest of all mortals.

The horses east of the mountains, which we have hitherto seen, are lazy, and without spirit; but hard usage and scanty fare may in a great degree account for their jaded appearance. Our followers tell us, that all the worn-out and otherwise useless horses are collected together and sent to what is called the "reserve," for the use of the Rocky Mountain pass. The California breed I found as superior to those of Columbia as the latter are to those we see here. Hence we might ask the question, Is there more Spanish blood in them? or does the horse deteriorate the further he goes to the north?

Having noticed the quality of our horses, we next come to our riding accoutrements. The bridle, if we may so call it, consists of a long thong of raw hide dressed in the country fashion, called Atscacha or Cubaress, some thirty feet long. One end of it is tied round the animal's lower jaw, the other, after running through the rider's left hand, passes over the animal, and drags on the ground some fifteen feet behind the horse. This is awkward when numbers are riding together among the whites, but pleasing to the Indian; because every jerk as the party moves along, causes the animal to rear and frolic about: this is looked upon as a mark of mettle, and shows a spirited animal, and the oftener the jerk is repeated by tramping on the atscacha, the more highly is the rider flattered, as it never fails to draw from him a smile of approbation. Awkward as the atscacha is, it comes finely into play when the rider has occasion to dismount, to shoot, or follow game, to tie his horse, or catch him when at liberty: in all these cases, it is far more handy than our bridle.

Next comes the saddle. It consists of a piece of dressed leather, made up in a peculiar fashion, and stuffed with grass or the hair of animals; with a broad and fringed crupper. The saddle is not unfrequently trimmed and handsomely ornamented with quill work, and the saddle cloth outdoes all the rest in tawdry ornaments; yet such is the construction of the Indian saddle, that it never fails to injure the horse's back: every horse carries his saddle-mark or sore back, as long as his legs carry him. Lastly, a piece of wood bent and shaped to hold the foot, supplies the place of the stirrup. The reader may now fancy the appearance of such a cavalcade parading the wilderness. Thus mounted, we generally started with the rising and encamped with the setting sun. Our horses being refreshed, we resumed our journey, and proceeding over the plain at a good speed soon reached Fort Edmonton, pleasantly situated on the north bank of the Saskatchewan River, a distance of one hundred miles from Fort Assiniboine.

Mr. Chief Factor Rowan, formerly a partner of the North-West Company, and long in the country, presides here as the chief man of what is called the Fort des Prairies, or Saskatchewan districts. By him we were received with open arms. Gentlemen in the service are in the habit of receiving all strangers, whether of high or low rank, connected or not with the Company, with courtesy and affability. From motives of interest all Indians visiting the establishments are welcomed with kindness, and treated as children by the traders. The habit becomes familiar to them, and they take a pleasure in holding out the right-hand of fellowship to all comers and goers.

On the evening we reached the fort, Mr. Rowan, according to custom, when a great man arrives, gave a grand ball in honour of Governor Simpson, at which all the people about the establishment, high and low, old and young of every class, attended, dressed in their best attire. I had often heard the females of Fort des Prairies celebrated for their attractions; and I must say that report had not in the least degree exaggerated their accomplishments. Modest and unassuming, they dressed well, danced well, and made a good show of fineries. In short, the whole entertainment was conducted with much good taste and decorum.

I had seen very few places in the country where

domestic arrangements, either within doors or without, were conducted with so much propriety as at this place. At almost every other post, men and women are to be seen congregating together during the sports and amusements of the men, and the women are often seen flirting idly about the establishments, mixing among the men at their several duties. But it is not so here: I did not notice a woman, old or young, married or single, going about the place idle; all seemed to keep at home, and to be employed about their own affairs. The moral and pleasing effect was such as might be expected, and reflects great credit on Mr. Rowan and on his family.

Fort Edmonton is a large compact establishment, with good buildings, palisades, and bastions, pleasantly situated in a deep valley. An extensive and profitable trade is carried on with the warlike tribes of the plains—Blackfeet, Piegans, Assiniboines, and Crees. All these roving bands look up to Mr. Rowan as their common father, and he has for more than a quarter of a century taught them to love and to fear him. Attached to this place are two large parks for raising grain, and, the soil being good, it produces large crops of barley and potatoes; but the spring and fall frosts prove injurious to wheat, which, in consequence, seldom comes to maturity

Adjoining the cultivated fields is a very fine level race-ground, of two miles or more in length;

horse-racing being one of the chief amusements of the place during the summer season: and here we may observe that Fort des Prairies is not only celebrated for fine women, but for fine horses. Mr. Rowan, a man of active habits, good humour, and fond of riding and racing as a pastime, keeps some of the best horses the country can produce, and we were favoured with a specimen of them. I rode round the race-ground a chestnut sixteen hands high, and very spirited. I must not fail to observe, after what has been already stated on the subject of horses, that many of them, both for size and muscle, were as fine animals as ever I had seen in the country; from which we were convinced that those belonging to what is called the "reserve" are not to be taken as a criterion for the whole country,—an instance how easily a careless observer might be deceived; for had we not seen Mr. Rowan's fine stud, we should have left the Saskatchewan with a very unfavourable opinion of the horses.

An abominable custom is very prevalent among the traders on this side the mountains, and Edmonton is entitled to its own share of odium —the keeping so many starving dogs about the establishment in summer for their imaginary services in winter. There were no less than fifty-two snarling and growling curs; and they are said to be very useful and profitable animals.

Formerly, during the days of opposition, dogs

might have been useful as runners, for the purpose of securing furs; but the peaceable state of the country now affords both time and convenience for the hunters to bring in their furs, and they do so: yet the dogs are still kept. During by-gone days the emulation among men for dogs as runners was so great that all their hard earnings were spent on them; and the tawdry paraphernalia required to ornament a first-rate train was as expensive as it was foolish: the wife might go without her blanket; but the husband must have his dogs, and the dogs their scarlet ribbons and their bells!

The custom, however reprehensible in this point of view, is equally so in others; for the nuisance of their presence in a fort is beyond endurance: they are the terror of every woman and child after dark. Nor can a stranger step from one door to another without being interrupted by them; and, worst of all, the place is kept like a kennel: in wet weather the horrid stench is intolerable.

These animals are in general of the wolf-breed, and are said to be vigorous and long-winded: a hundred miles a-day is a common journey for them. They are not generally reared about the establishments, but purchased from the natives for a mere trifle when young: when trained, they sell among the whites as high as five pounds sterling—double the price of a horse—and sometimes higher, according to fancy.

From Edmonton a brigade of boats makes a trip to York Factory and back once every year, carrying out the annual stock of furs, and bringing back the supplies required for the trade: this trip generally takes four months and a half to perform. We had to wait the spring arrangements, and before they were completed fourteen days had elapsed; at the end of that period, however, the flotilla, consisting of twelve barges, started with us on board; and we enjoyed a very pleasant voyage down the broad and swift Saskatchewan.

The boats in this quarter are considerably larger and stronger built than those in use on the Columbia. New boats here will cost twenty-five pounds sterling. They are propelled with oars, are roomy and comfortable, and carry from eighty to one hundred pieces, of a hundred pounds weight each. We descended this delightful stream with high water, fair wind, and full sails; the river being smooth, and free from rapids, but not in all places free from sand-bars. The land on each side rises gradually from the water's edge, and recedes as gradually back to the height of the last bank in a green undulating surface of hill and dale, to a considerable distance; then the country opens finely to view, presenting a plain of almost boundless extent. This place has neither the bold and rocky shores, nor the wild and mountainous aspect, of Columbia, but has been well termed the land of prairies—a land teeming with buffalo and deer, lakes and wild fowl; and for diversity of landscape, or beauty of scenery, few countries can equal—none surpass it. We continued our voyage until we reached Carlton: general course, east; distance, three hundred and eighty miles. We occasionally observed on the heights, as we sailed along, some straggling bands of Indians, but met with none of them.

Carlton House is built on the south bank, about one hundred and fifty yards from the water side; behind which is a rising ground, which commands the place. This establishment is next in extent and importance to Edmonton. It was at this time, however, undergoing a thorough repair, and had a very unfavourable appearance. The river, which is here broad, and the opposite side agreeable, presents a most delightful prospect in front. The south side, however, as well as the east and west, have nothing to boast of: high ground, covered with dwarf poplar, confines the view.

Detached bands of the same warlike tribes who frequent Edmonton trade also at this place; but furs are rapidly declining. The trade is not considered profitable; and the Indians are not at all times friendly. The Crees alone, who inhabit the country to the north, are quiet and friendly; those on the south are brigands. In summer a guard by day and a watch by night are indispensable; and the hostile visitors have been known to scalp some of the whites within a hundred yards of the fort gate.

Carlton, like many other places in this country, has too often changed masters to be what it ought to be—a compact and formidable establishment, so necessary where hostile Indians frequent. The palisades are neither straight nor strong, two very great faults in fortifying against Indians; and over the front gate is a paltry sort of bastion, or blockhouse, in which few would venture to fire a pistol. Altogether, the place had neither strength nor beauty to recommend it; and at the time we arrived ten resolute Indians might have taken it with the greatest ease.

There are, however, some good cultivated fields, which, with moderate industry, are said to yield abundant crops of barley and potatoes. Wheat grows here, and hops have been raised with great success; the gardens also produce good returns of onions, carrots, turnips, and cabbages. And here I noticed the best root-houses I have seen in the country. It is pleasing thus to witness the fruits of industry and progress of civilisation in the savage wilderness. Among the associations of this place many stories exist, and many funny anecdotes are told; but as we do not profess to give a history of the place, but merely a remark or two on it, we shall notice but one. A gentleman, in preparing for his rambles and amusements out of doors, set about making a fancy carriage in-doors, and, the better to guard the work from injury and the varnish from stains, he would have it done in one of his private rooms; but, in doing so, he unluckily forgot to notice that the door, which admitted the materials piecemeal, would not let out the vehicle as a whole! So there it remained—a ludicrous *miscarriage*.

After a stay of four days we left Carlton; and, if we except the kindness of our good old friend Chief Factor Stuart, we saw nothing else about the place, either to awaken admiration or lessen the pleasure we felt on leaving it to resume our voyage. Some distance from Carlton, as we descended the river, the high lands and wide-spreading plains gave place gradually to a country less and less pleasing to the eye; although the stream itself increases in magnitude, and is smooth and free from rapids. This unfavourable change may be considered the commencement of what is called the Mis-Keegoe or swampy country—a land of lakes, morasses, and quagmires. As we descended, we fell in with a small band of Crees; and being the first camp of Indians I had seen in this quarter, I naturally drew a comparison between them and those I had been accustomed to west of the mountains. To me the contrast appeared very striking: the former, humble and abject, approached us with a bland smile, and cringing familiarity;

whereas the rude Columbians never accost the whites but with an air of imperious contempt, which is natural to them.

The Crees have none of that stern and forbidding look peculiar to some tribes west of the mountains: the open and pleasing smile of familiarity is in their countenances. They are broader built, larger about the shoulders, have broader faces and larger feet than the lank Columbians; but they are not so straight, have an awkward gait, and stoop forward when they walk. The only article these poor creatures offered us for sale was a few small bags of feathers—an article I had never seen for sale among Indians before. From what we could learn, this part of the country is almost ruined in the more profitable article of furs, and most animals of the chase are getting further off every day; which circumstance has thrown the natives almost entirely on the produce of the waters for their living. The further we advanced the more gloomy, wet, and swampy the country became, until we reached the next halting-place, called Cumberland House. General course, north-east; distance from Carlton, two hundred and sixty miles.

Fort Cumberland is situated at the south end of Sturgeon Lake, where fish of that name is taken in great abundance; they are very fine and well-flavoured, although small in comparison to those caught on the Columbia; the largest generally taken here not exceeding seventy pounds. This establishment is large and tolerably well built, with a handsome dwelling-house, having glass windows, and what is still more uncommon in these parts, a gallery in front—the only instance of the kind I have yet seen in the country. Here James Leith, Esq., one of the oldest partners of the North-West, and senior chief factor in the Hudson's Bay service, presided as chief manager of the department. The trade of the place is, however, fast dwindling away to nothing; but in proportion as furs and animals of the chase are decreasing, agriculture seems to be increasing, and perhaps eventually the latter may prove to the natives more beneficial than the former.

In addition to the cultivated fields, we have to notice here the cheering prospect of domestic comfort. The introduction of domestic cattle from the colony of Red River gives a new feature of civilisation to the place. Here are two fine milch cows and a bull, and more are expected. In addition to these, other proofs of industry and comfort are manifest. A neat kitchen-garden, which furnishes an ample supply of vegetables, adorns the place, in the centre of which stands a sun-dial neatly cut and figured; the latitude of the place, 53° 57′ N., being marked on it.

Cumberland is, however, a gloomy place. Here we found the advanced party of Franklin's northern expedition waiting for orders. After a week's delay, we embarked to pursue our voyage.

The river, as we descended, loses much of its majestic appearance, owing to the bends it takes in its course; which led us round almost to every point of the compass, until we made Lake Bourbon, commonly called Cedar Lake, from the timber found along its shores. Here the first adventurers from Canada built an establishment called Fort Bourbon, which gives the name to the lake; but no traces of a fort now exist: it also denotes the extent of the discoveries made by the French, on the line from Montreal, prior to the taking of Quebec by the English in 1759.

This lake, although not very large, is subject to a heavy swell, owing probably to the water being shallow. The west side is rocky and high, with wood all round it. All the lakes in this quarter produce abundance of white fish; but they are not all of equally good quality. In some the fish are much larger, firmer, and of superior quality; and this is said to be one of them.

Just as we got out of Lake Bourbon, we met Captain Franklin and Dr. Richardson on their overland Arctic expedition, making all the haste possible to join their friends at Cumberland. We breakfasted with them; and after passing about an hour together, bade each other good-bye, and parted; they starting for the west, and we for the east. This lake led us into Cross Lake, from thence we soon reached the Grand Rapid, where a portage had to be made, at the foot of which the great

Saskatchewan loses itself in the wide-spreading Winipeg. The whole route, from Cumberland to this place, some twenty-five or thirty leagues, is low boggy ground, and goes under the general appellation of the Swampy Country.

The Grand Rapid is the only bad step in the Saskatchewan, from Edmonton to Lake Winipeg. Here we fell in with another small party of the Cree nation, called Mis-Keegoes or Swampies, employed in killing sturgeon, which appeared to be of the same size and quality as those of Sturgeon Lake. These Indians were civil and kind, but badly clothed, and appeared very poor; having something to eat, there was a smile of contentment on every countenance. The females were partly clad in European articles; but the garments of the men were of the produce of the chase.

From the Grand Rapid we coasted along the west side of the barren and rocky shore of Lake Winipeg. In this range there is a jutting point, or peninsula, which runs out boldly for some considerable distance into the lake, and is called Mossy Point; the voyageur often doubles this point with apprehension, as there is no way of getting on shore to save either boats or cargoes in case of a storm, and it is at all times exposed to the fury of the waves. Mossy Point is therefore called the Cape Horn of Lake Winipeg. After clearing the point, we coasted along until we reached our next halting-place, at the north end of the lake, called

Norway House. General course, east; distance from Cumberland, two hundred miles.

From the source of the Saskatchewan to this place, a distance of some nine hundred miles in length, the natives in former days were very numerous; as much so, as they are now the reverse. The north side of the river is occupied principally by the Crees, who, of all the Indians, were once the most numerous and powerful; being superior in individual intelligence, and distinguished alike for sagacity and mildness of disposition. Of this vast and powerful tribe, the scanty remains are in a condition as abject and wretched as their forefathers were independent and happy. Their wilderness scenery is still the same; their mountains, lakes, and rivers present the same aspect as they did centuries ago; and their prairies and forests are green as ever, while the wretched inhabitants are fast dying away.

The country on the south side of the river, all the way to the Missouri, is inhabited by a number of mixed and roving tribes, bold in war, and wild as their own native lands; and, with the exception of the Blackfeet, Piegans, and Assiniboines, who still retain their national character, they are little better known than by name. With regard to the actual number of any one of these tribes, or of the whole of them taken together, it is impossible to form any correct estimate; nor even can the boundaries of territory which each tribe claims as its own, be strictly defined.

When I was on the Missouri, I was told that the Blackfeet and Piegans who frequent that quarter, mustered together fifteen hundred lodges; and while passing through the Saskatchewan, I have been also told that those of the same tribes who visit and trade there, mustered one thousand lodges; but those of the Missouri and Saskatchewan mix together. Now allowing six to each lodge or tent, the aggregate number would be fifteen thousand five hundred individuals.

We have noticed on our route the commencement of agriculture and the introduction of domestic cattle at Cumberland House. From Edmonton down to Carlton, and far below, a range of five hundred miles, the country and climate invite the husbandman and the plough, and if the system now introduced be followed up with energy and success, the natives will doubtless profit by it; so that a remnant of that almost extinct, and degraded race, may yet be saved; for the Crees are a mild, docile, and half-civilised people. But the introduction of agriculture, however beneficial to the natives, must eventually prove ruinous to the interests of the Company, as by it the Indians will be taught habits of industry and attachment to a locality, and learn from example and experience the useful lesson that the cultivation of the soil is a more certain resource than the chase. And when once they are drawn by motives of interest and gratification to farming, they will be useless to the

Company in a commercial point of view; for the Indians are the sinews of their trade. What a noble and praiseworthy instance of self-denial we have in the conduct of men sacrificing their own interests to benefit others! We, therefore, wish the principle thus begun may be carried out and become general, not only on the Saskatchewan, but everywhere else throughout their territories. There is but one inference to be drawn, namely, that it has been introduced chiefly to benefit the natives; and the laudable undertaking will no doubt, in the end, be crowned with a successful result.

As Mr. Leith of Cumberland, one of the warmest hearted and most philanthropic gentlemen in this or any other country, emphatically observed to me, while talking about the poverty of the Indians and the introduction of agriculture among them, "It is a plan introduced at the eleventh hour; but better late than never." I saw at once he was a man of feeling, and a friend to the Indian; and I showed him a few hasty opinions that I had thrown together on the subject. We then compared notes, and met each other's objections by a comparison between the natives west and east of the Rocky Mountains. After some further conversation, Mr. Leith opened his mind to me freely. Indeed, I could see that if he did not alleviate the condition of the natives, it was not the will but the power that was wanting. He was a man well advanced in life, of strict integrity, and of a religious turn of mind.

"The fur trade in these parts," remarked he, "is dwindling away to nothing: the returns even now scarcely cover the expenses; and shall we, after ruining the country and the natives to enrich ourselves, leave no other memento behind us but desolation and death? Half a century ago, this country was rich in furs and animals of the chase, the natives were numerous, independent, and happy; but now, alas! natives, and riches, and happiness have almost disappeared from the face of this and other parts of the country." "And where," continued he, "are all those among ourselves, who basked in the sunshine of a lucrative trade during that short period? Gone, like the natives themselves, to the land of forgetfulness; and with scarcely a solitary instance of one who did not outlive his means; so that nothing now remains of all their labour under the sun." I inferred at once, from what he said, although he expressed nothing more than I have stated, that he intended to do something for the destitute natives.

The year after this, Mr. Leith left the country for the last time and went home; on his way out, I happened to meet him at Norway House, and we journeyed together to York Factory. Some years afterwards we learned that he had left by his will* 10,000*l.* sterling for the religious instruction of the Indians.

* See Appendix.

¹ NOTE.—After a lapse of ten years, and after protracted litigation, the trustees of Mr. Leith's will were enabled, in the year 1848, to set apart £10,000 towards the endowment of a bishopric in Prince Rupert's Land.

We have annexed an extract from the will for the information of our readers; leaving with them a decision on the many conflicting opinions respecting the intentions of the testator. His benevolence and desire to Christianise the Indians are placed beyond doubt.

EXTRACT from the Will of JAMES LEITH, ESQ., of York Factory, Hudson's Bay (late of Torquay).

"I give, devise, and bequeath the remaining moiety or half-part of my lands, heritages, personal estate, and effects not hereinbefore disposed of by this my Will, unto my brother, the said William Hay Leith, and his heirs, the Lord Bishop of London for the time being, the Reverend the Dean of Westminster for the time being, and the Governor and Deputy-Governor, for the time being, of the Hudson's Bay Company, upon the trusts, and for the ends, intents, and purposes following: that is to say, upon trust that the said William Hay Leith and his heirs, the Lord Bishop of London for the time being, the Dean of Westminster for the time being, and the Governor and Deputy-Governor, for the time being, of the Hudson's Bay Company, as aforesaid, do and shall with all convenient speed convert the whole thereof into money, and lay out and invest the same in their names in the public stocks or funds of Great Britain, at interest, and do and shall, from time to time, expend, lay out, and dispose of the interest, dividends, and annual proceeds arising therefrom, in such manner as to them, or the majority of them, shall seem most desirable and advantageous for the purpose of establishing, propagating, and extending the Christian Protestant religion in and amongst the native aboriginal Indians in that part of America formerly called Rupert's Land, but now more generally known by the name of the Hudson's Bay Territory. I beg here to remark, that I do not consider the neighbourhood of a colony a fit place for the commencement of such a work; but I wish it to be understood as an observation only, as I must leave it to the above-mentioned Trustees to act according to their own opinions, guided by existing circumstances; and I trust they will do so as men of honour and understanding."

Will dated 20th February, 1835.

Testator died 19th June, 1838.

Will proved by the Executors in the Prerogative Court Canterbury, 11th August, 1838. Property valued under £9000.

CHAPTER XVI.

Nelson River—Route to York Factory—Norway House—Climate—Great rendezvous—Governor Simpson—Annual councils—The fur trade—Remarks on the present system—The Governor's unlimited power—General remarks—My own final arrangements—Retiring servants—Leave Norway House—Qualities of our boat's crew—Physical deformities—A canoe hero—Account of his life—The voyageur's paradise—More words than work—Gloomy prospects—Dreary shore—Useless hands—Spider Islands—Poplar Islands—The storm—Narrow escape—Stormy Island—Squalls—Second storm—Gale on the lake—Boat aground—Danger—Confusion—Boat high and dry—The stormy night—Beren's River—The lop-stick—Grand view of the lake—Cat-Fish Creek—Dog's Head—Anticipations—Plans and projects—Story of a night's adventures—Devout voyageurs—Saints invoked—The solemn vow—The mysterious lights—The two channels—Grindstone Point—Drunken River—Arrive at the mouth of Red River—Lake Winipeg and its feeders—Navigation—Start for the Metropolis—The Public Road—Image Plains—Currency—Frog Plains—Civilization and Barbarism—Geographical Position—Speculations—Fort Garry, the Metropolis—A day in Red River.

WE have noticed our arrival at Norway House, situated at the northern extremity of Winipeg, where issues the Nelson River, a stream of considerable magnitude, running, in a north-easterly direction, through a rugged rocky country, and falling into the sea at Port Nelson, in Hudson's Bay. Although a number of large and small streams fall into Lake Winipeg, yet the Nelson River is the only outlet from it, and is one of the routes to York Factory, but not the one generally followed by the voyageurs. The other, and the common route, is by descending this river to the distance of about twenty miles, and then ascending a small stream, which falls into it, as far as the height of land named the "Painted Stone," from certain figures carved and painted on it by the Indians, and where they formerly left some offerings to propitiate the deity of the place. On the east side of this height of land there is a chain of small lakes, out of which Hay's River takes its source, and, after passing through a barren uneven country intersected by some lakes and rivers, discharges itself into the sea at York Factory, in latitude 57° 2' north, and longitude 92° 36' west.

In the neighbourhood of Norway House there is a small river, which, according to report, was entered, during the time of the French, by a trader of the name of Perrault, about the year 1740, and named by him Pointe du Nord. It was afterwards called Rivière aux Brochet, or Pike River, from the abundance of these fish found in its waters; from which circumstance, also, the first establishment here was named Fort Brochet, and bore that name until a few years ago, when it was changed from

Fort Brochet to Norwegian Point. A number of Norwegians were hired by the late Earl of Selkirk, and were sent to that point for the purpose of clearing the woods and making a winter road to York Factory, but the project was found to be impracticable, and was therefore abandoned; hence the place was called Norwegian Point, and from Norwegian Point the factory is called Norway House.

During the year the place was by accident burnt to the ground, and at the time of my writing it lay in ashes. Preparations were in progress for rebuilding it on a more extensive scale, a little further down the river, on a rocky point, near to a place called the Play Green Lake. I should not be surprised if another name is given to the new establishment, for the people of this country are whimsical in giving new names to old places, and think little of changing them. Vegetation here dares hardly raise its head; the gleams of summer—if, in these forlorn regions, there be any summer—are rapidly chased away by the blasts of autumn, which again as rapidly flee before the storms of winter. The soil seldom produces anything in perfection.

Norway House is a place of considerable business and bustle during the summer season. It is the great inland rendezvous of the fur trade in this quarter. Here the people and returns of all the trading posts belonging to the Company, from Lake Superior on the south, the Rocky Mountains on the west, and the Frozen Ocean on the north, are collected together once a year, on their way to York Factory. Norway House would, therefore, be a fit place for a missionary station. Although people from all quarters muster here, yet none of those scenes of carousing and fighting, for which Fort William and other places were so celebrated, disgrace the meeting of friends. Peace, sobriety, and good order have put an end to those demoralising scenes which formerly disgraced human nature in this country. There are likewise but few of the French Canadians now in the service: those favourite children of the north-west school.

This brings us to the fur trade, the all-absorbing pursuit in the country over which the Company holds sway. These territories may be divided into four great sections,—the northern and southern departments of Rupert's Land, the Columbia District, and the King's Posts, as they are called; divisions each of them ample enough in extent for the territory of a crowned head. Once a year the Governor-in-chief, as the superintending officer is styled, generally makes his tour through the greater part of these wild dominions, holding his annual council at the head quarters of each department, and assembling round him, on each occasion, all the commissioned functionaries, the factors and traders within convenient reach. There the business of the departments is investigated and the requisite appointments are made; in short, it is there that the various arrangements are settled for conducting affairs at the different posts within their jurisdiction.

Few men in this country ever possessed such authority as does Governor Simpson, the Company's present representative; and none, we believe, ever gave more general satisfaction. Courteous in his manners, and active in his habits; gifted in a high degree with the power of self-command, and above all with a keen discernment of character; he appears eminently fitted by the union of these qualities for the commanding station which he so ably fills.

The extent of country over which Governor Simpson presides, stretches from the Atlantic to the Pacific: there is no place in all the vast wilderness that he has not visited; every spot in it is known to him; there is scarcely a native but at some time or other has experienced his smile and his liberality. His fostering care has been over all.

We have paid some attention to the working of the present system in all its parts, and it does not appear to us, under all circumstances, that a change in any way could be made that would hold out a prospect of improving the trade or bettering the condition of the natives; everything seems to be done that can be done; therefore, any change from the present mode of governing the country might do more harm than good: even the monopoly itself, if removed, might be ruinous to the aboriginal inhabitants. It has been said that all monopolies are illegal restraints on freedom; to this general rule, however, there are exceptions. The monopoly is the best guarantee the natives of Rupert's Land have that the country will not be the prey of lawless strife; unless it were placed under the fostering care of a good and vigilant government.

It not unfrequently happens that the Council meets at other places, as well as at head quarters; indeed, wherever it is convenient for the Governor to attend. The Council of the northern department was held at Norway House this year, instead of at York Factory. During the sittings, which only occupy a few days, no other business is attended to; but the Council no sooner breaks up, than matters of minor importance are looked into. Each factor, trader, and post-master then sets about preparing and forwarding the business of his own especial charge.

When the public business was over, the Governor sent for me, and I repaired to his room. He received me courteously, according to his custom. After some conversation, he adverted to the subject of my remaining in the country, and continuing my former pursuits. "If you remain in the service," said he, "you shall have the entire management of the Company's affairs in the Snake country guaranteed to you for a certain number of years, with a liberal salary." I tendered my thanks for his handsome offer, but declined accepting it, urging as a reason that I had already twice tried the fur trade, and had twice been disappointed in my expectations; and, therefore, if experience was worth anything, I ought not any longer to reject its warnings; but, above all, I urged as my strongest motive for leaving the service, the necessity of retiring to a place where I could have the means of giving my children a Christian education, the best portion I could leave them.

After a short pause, the Governor observed, "Well, although you are determined on leaving the service, I am still disposed to be your friend: what can I do for you?" I answered, "Your Excellency has always been a friend to me, and if you are still disposed to add another favour to those I have already received, grant me a spot of land in Red River, that I can call my own, and I shall be very thankful." "Your request shall be granted," said he, "and the Company, in consideration of your exertions and success in the Snake country, are disposed to add something to it." On this occasion, I had every reason to be satisfied. He sent for the chief accountant, and ordered him to draw up a deed for a hundred acres of land, free of all expense, which he signed, handed to me, and we parted.

At Norway House we had to remain for more than a week, before the bustle of public business was over; and another week almost passed before we could get a boat's crew mustered, out of the invalid class ejected from the service. All the infirm and superannuated servants of the Company are taken from the different posts and left at Norway House, to be conveyed to their respective countries; or they are allowed to take up their abode in Red River. It happened this year that several of the invalids were destined for Red River, and very anxious to get on. Hearing that I was on my way thither, rather than wait the Company's regular conveyance they applied for a passage with me, and promised to work their way. I looked at them for some time, and certainly as far as appearances went they seemed to be worthless. "What can you do?" asked I of one of them. "Sir, I can do anything: I can steer, row, and sail; I have been brought up to the voyage." "And you," said I to another, "what can you do?" "I have been a steersman for five years," replied he. "And you," pointing to a third, "what have you been?" "We are all boatmen," was his reply. Indeed, they boasted so much of what they had done and could do, that I overlooked their age, and took six of them at their word. So we prepared to leave Norway House. In our company was a Mr. Bird and his family, which augmented our number to twenty-seven persons; all of whom, as well as myself, were bound for the same destination, and had taken a last farewell of the service. Embarking, therefore, on Lake Winipeg, we turned our faces towards Red River, hoisted sail, and proceeded on our voyage.

And as it may be interesting to the reader to know something of the character of these superannuated sons of the wilderness, we shall sketch them. In the first place, then, three of them were able to help themselves, if not others; but as for the other three, their day was gone by: all of them were poor, more or less mutilated, infirm, and clogged with large families. But they were, nevertheless, very talkative, and independent in their way—North-Westers to the backbone; they had long yarns to tell of their past lives, as all voyageurs have, and were full of life and spirits.

Of this motley crew, we shall notice some striking peculiarities in the more aged and experienced of them: one was blind of an eye, and lame from having been frost-bitten; another was a cripple from the same cause; and a third had lost his thumb by accident. The last of this trio, the patriarchal head, had reached the wrong side of seventy years; and his wife, from infirmity, walked on crutches; but the froward old man, still active for his age, was as waggish and thoughtless as a youth of fifteen.

One day, while in a jocular mood, the old man began to talk over his past life: it was full of adventure, and may appear amusing to others, as it did to us. I shall give it, as nearly as I can, in his own words.

"I have now," said he, "been forty-two years in this country. For twenty-four I was a light canoe-man; I required but little sleep, but sometimes got less than I required. No portage was too long for me; all portages were alike. My end of the canoe never touched the ground till I saw the end of it. Fifty songs a day were nothing to me. I could carry, paddle, walk, and sing with any man I ever saw. During that period, I saved the lives of ten Bourgeois, and was always the favourite, because when others stopped to carry at a bad step, and lost time, I pushed on—over rapids, over cascades, over chûtes; all were the same to me. No water, no weather, ever stopped the paddle or the song. I have had twelve wives in the country; and was once possessed of fifty horses, and six running dogs, trimmed in the first style. I was then like a Bourgeois, rich and happy: no Bourgeois had better-dressed wives than I; no Indian chief finer horses; no white man better-harnessed or swifter dogs. I beat all Indians at the race, and no white man ever passed me in the chase. I wanted for nothing; and I spent all my earnings in the enjoyment of pleasure. Five hundred pounds, twice told, have passed through my hands; although now I have not a spare shirt to my back, nor a penny to buy one. Yet, were I young again, I should glory in commencing the same career again. I would pend another half-century in the same fields of enjoyment. There is no life so happy as a voyageur's life; none so independent; no place where a man enjoys so much variety and freedom as in the Indian country. Huzza! huzza! pour le pays sauvage!" After this *cri de joie*, he sat down in the boat, and we could not help admiring the wild enthusiasm of the old Frenchman. He had boasted and excited himself, till he was out of breath, and then sighed with regret that he could no longer enjoy the scenes of his past life.

The life of this hero may serve as an index to that of the others: their history was of a similar tenour. Their long-winded stories were of little use in propelling our boat through Lake Winipeg. Their habits of indolence and thoughtlessness, which but little agreed with the character they had given of themselves, could not be overcome. Nothing could stimulate them to perseverance. They could smoke, sing, and rehearse the most fabulous adventures of their own lives; but they could not guide the helm, ply the oar, or trim the sail: so that we had to creep along the barren and rocky shores of Winipeg. We have given our readers a brief sketch of the life and habits of an old voyageur, and a true picture of our crew.

It would, however, be unfair to judge all the voyageurs by the example of poverty and depravity before us. Instances are not wanting of the old and retiring voyageurs leaving the country hale and hearty, with their pockets lined with the fruits of industry, and their character untainted with vice.

All this time our bark was speeding her way to the south. We had started with a sail wind; but it soon died away, and we had to ply the oar under a hot sun, and got on but slowly. Our course lay along the eastern shore, whose character is low and rocky. Not a harbour or creek invited the tiny craft to a friendly shelter until we reached the Spider Islands, a small rocky group lying out in the lake, ten miles from our starting point, where we found a safe and convenient harbour. These small islands, although very little higher than the blue lake that surrounds them, shelter the voyageur from every wind.

From Spider Islands we steered our course across a broad traverse for Poplar Islands, a distance of ten miles more. Here the channel, narrow and intricate, passes between a cluster of rocks and the main land. This place we reached under easy sail, a little before sunset; but instead of encamping there, as we ought to have done, we undertook at that late hour to cross another still broader bay, stretching to a place called Colony Point. We had soon reason to regret our imprudence; for we had scarcely gone half a mile, when the sky grew red, and the wind, veering from north to west, blew a gale, and forced us into the bay. Here nothing was to be seen before us but a chain of rocks, over which the breakers rushed with a violence that threatened instant destruction. Our boat speeding through the water, and the sun setting at the time, added to our terror.

At this moment I perceived on our right something like an island; but we were then passing it. Pointing to the object, I called to the man at the helm to make for the island. "Impossible," said he; "the boat will swamp." "Swamp or sink," said I, "there is no other hope for us." Calling a man to the sheet, which I was then holding, I sprang back to the helm, and brought up the boat almost broadside to the wind, in order to gain the island; but, in doing so, we had a very narrow escape: two or three heavy waves breaking over us, almost sent us to the bottom. I still kept her head for the island, as a last resource; but the crew seconded my endeavours very feebly: they lost all presence of mind, and, in their confusion, let go the sail! What followed was a struggle between life and death. Those men who had but a short time before boasted so much of their skill and prowess among lakes, now abandoned their posts and began to count their beads and cross themselves: only one man stood at his duty; yet Providence favoured us, and we reached the island in safety. It proved so small, that the waves from each side met in the lee with such violence, as to threaten us with instant destruction. We got on the rocks with the utmost difficulty; and fortunate it was, for had we run into the bay, no earthly power could have saved us.

I had now a specimen of the skill of my crew. They were all boatmen a few days before; but when I reminded them of their boasting, they justified themselves by saying, "We have had more experience in canoes than boats;" adding, however, "we never had a narrower escape." So boisterous was the weather, that we were kept prisoners on the island for two days, before we could venture on the water again. I need scarcely say that there was an end to all boasting. As soon as we had left the island, and resumed our voyage, I reminded my men of their late conduct, to prepare them for another time; but they did not half like it. The youngsters—even the women—teased them. But the poor fellows were completely humbled, and tried to avoid the subject. It put an end to all self-conceit, for after that we had less talk and more work.

After leaving our rocky retreat, the coast continued in appearance much the same as before, here and there marked with jutting points and bays, with a low beach composed of sand and gravel. The bays, although not large, form in their circuit many miles in length. In order, therefore, to save time and diminish labour, we steered in a direct line from point to point. Notwithstanding the narrow escapes we had met with by venturing too far out, my men were very anxious to avoid as much as possible the fatigue of the oar; and the canoe hero exclaimed, "There is as much difference between the nimble paddle and the drawling oar as between youth and old age." Most voyageurs in this country are as averse to boats as they are partial to canoes, and as awkward in the former as they are adroit in the latter.

The third day after leaving Stormy Island, as we were gliding across a bay from Beren's River to Pigeon Point, with a light breath of wind, scarcely sufficient to indicate the quarter from whence it came, the sky clear and weather fine, we were warned of danger by the appearance of a dark cloud and heavy gale coming from the west. It approached us with a noise like thunder, and with the quickness of lightning. The placid surface of the lake around us was, in an instant, turned into a sheet of fire, leaving us scarcely a moment to prepare for it. The gale struck the boat, and wheeled her round. Such was its violence, that the men were thrown down from their seats, and the boat driven to the bottom of the bay, where it lay among the rocks and stones, high on the beach, without our receiving any other injury than that of a fright; for on approaching the shore, the boat stuck fast on a sand-bar, till one or two heavy waves passed over her, when with the next she fortunately floated, and carried us high up on the beach, where we effected a landing. The moment the boat struck on the bank, the confusion was equal to the danger, wives grasping their husbands, husbands their children; but no one thought of the boat, the only thing that could save us.

When the wind had abated and the water subsided to its natural level, we found ourselves more than thirty yards from the water's edge, high and dry. Here we had to pass the night, fireless, sleepless, and shelterless, under a torrent of rain; and the floating of the boat next day took us six hours. This affair taught us to avoid all traverses; and the old fellows, thankful for their deliverance, took to their oars in good earnest, fully determined to keep along shore. Near the mouth of Beren's River, opposite to this place, the Company have a trading-post. In passing it, however, we saw no Indians. Here are also a few small islands, which give to this part of the lake a pleasing effect: on one of them a fine tall pine, trimmed into a maypole, with its broom head, was conspicuous at a distance. One of my men, pointing to it, observed, "That's a lop-stick I trimmed eighteen years ago."

Pigeon Point, and all the vicinity, is well clothed with pine timber; but in other respects the rocky aspect continues, and the land is very little higher than the water. Yet from this position we had a good view of the lake, where it is at its greatest breadth, I should say about thirty-five miles, and it spreads out towards the west like an ocean. But the water is very shallow, the bottom rocky, and the beach full of stones. When the wind blows from the west, sailing is difficult, so that we got on exceedingly slow, taking three days from Pigeon Point to Cat-fish Creek; which, under favourable circumstances, we might have done in as many hours. Cat-fish Creek is a safe little harbour; I should say one of the best on the lake. Here we encamped for the night, being our twelfth day on the lake. A light breeze springing up, we sailed before daylight, and were soon at Rabbit Point; and from thence crossed a deep bay to a place called the Dog's Head. The lake becomes narrow in this part; the east side still more rocky and barren, with stunted pines; and the west side, for the first time, sufficiently near to show a rugged and broken surface, with a bold and rocky shore.

All these huge rocks and solitary islands afford dry and safe halting-places to numerous aquatic birds.

At the Dog's Head we considered ourselves out of all danger, the land on either side being within our reach; so we encamped in a snug little harbour, just large enough for our boat, and no more. We had no sooner put up for the night, than the thought of soon reaching their destination so cheered and animated the crew, that they passed the evening cracking their jokes and forming new plans and projects for enjoying life in Red River. One observed, "I will have my house built with double rooms;" another, "I will have my rooms ceiled and painted." It was really amusing to hear men without a shilling in the world enjoying life in their airy dreams, where nothing was real. One of the party related a night's adventures in this place, a few years before, in going with a boat from Fort Alexander to Jack River. His account was as follows:—

"We encamped at dusk one evening in this place; but the little harbour not proving safe, owing to the direction of the wind, we took supper, and then embarked again to look out for a place of greater safety. We had scarcely got out on the lake, and the sail up, before the atmosphere became overcast; the thunder was heavy, lightning flashes were frequent, and the night was very dark. We tried with all haste to get back to land again; but before we could get the sail down or the boat turned, the wind shifted and blew a gale from the land, accompanied with a deluge of rain. In this moment of peril we took to our oars, in the hope of being able to regain the land; but all our endeavours proved fruitless: the state of the weather prevented us from using our oars to advantage; some of us were pulling backward as often as forward. At length no alternative remained but to submit to the mercy of the winds and waves; and unfortunately both were against us.

"From the appearance of the opposite shore before dark, we considered that we could not have been more than five or six miles from it; but from its bold and rocky aspect, to have approached it with the wind that then blew would leave us little hope;

to hoist sail and keep to the right, to avoid the rocks, was equally dangerous, for in that case, nothing but the open lake was before us; rocks and islands were everywhere around us.

"Circumstances, however, decided for us: the boat, no longer able to resist, was every moment in danger of being swamped; so we resolved on hoisting sail: it was with great exertion that we got it half-mast high, and then keeping the boat to the left as much as possible, we preferred to run the risk of the opposite shore to the open lake on the right. Some baled out the water, while others kept a sharp look-out, which amounted to nothing; for except the lightning flashed, no one could see another in the boat, and we every moment fancied we heard the rush of waves dashing on the rocks ahead of us. Some said they saw the rocks, and called to prepare for the danger: death stared us in the face.

"In the midst of this confusion a strange phenomenon appeared: a meteor of fire, resembling a lighted candle, settled on the left end of the yardarm. Supposing it to have been fire communicated by the lightning, we secured our guns under the covering; this done, another light settled on the right end of the yard, and immediately afterwards another showed itself on the top of the mast. The lights were rather pale, and of a reddish hue. All the three continued bright and steady for more than half an hour, without shifting; nor had the rain, the thunder, or the lightning the least effect on any of them. At length they dropped off and disappeared: first that on the left, then the one on the right, and lastly, the one on the mast-head.

"This extraordinary appearance so terrified us that we could scarcely utter a word; when suddenly we were startled by the boat entering among bushes, where it soon afterwards grounded. Grasping the bushes, we held fast till daylight brought us relief. In our anxiety to keep among the friendly bushes, we thought of nothing else but self-preservation; and while thus engaged, the agitation of the water and working of the boat unshipped the rudder, which we lost, as well as two oars and some articles of clothing. The wind still continued to blow hard, but the thunder and rain moderated.

"In our adventures we had only reached the opposite side of the narrows, not more than six miles from whence we started; although we had been tossing on the water a great part of the night, and expected we had been driven at least thirty miles, and that we were in the middle of the lake: we must have been turning round and round. And that saved us; for had we been driven on shore fifty yards to the left of where we were, instead of willows we must have come in contact with bold naked rocks; or, had we been some three hundred yards further to the right, we must have missed the opposite shore of the narrows altogether, and found ourselves out in the open lake, where we might have been driven fifty miles without meeting with land. On either hand our case would have been hopeless.

"When daylight disclosed to us our situation, we had every reason to be thankful, for the stem of the boat was within twenty yards of the rocks. But the three lights frightened us the most. Some said it was two of the Apostles, Peter and Paul, guarding the Virgin Mary; others, that the appearance was ominous, and presaged that three of us would be drowned; while some said that only three out of the nine who were in the boat would survive the storm. We then knelt down, took our rosaries, and ran over our Ave-Marias and Paternosters; praying, some to one saint, some to another: I prayed to the Virgin Mary. This done, we made a solemn vow, that if we lived to see a priest we would have a grand mass offered up as a thanksgiving to the Virgin Mary for our miraculous deliverance."

Here I interrupted him, and asked which of the saints he thought saved them. "The Virgin Mary," replied he; "and I have always been anxious to get to Red River to perform my vow and get a grand mass said before I die: some of the others have already paid the debt of nature without seeing a priest, but I hope to be more fortunate." And this ended the story of his nocturnal adventures, which he said he never could forget as long as he lived.

Vows of this kind are always religiously observed by old voyageurs. As to the three tapers, I have more than once witnessed the same phenomenon when sailing in dark nights in stormy weather, but never observed the lights settle on either the mast or yard-arm, except during storms of thunder and lightning; and although the flame appeared fully as large and bright as that of a burning candle, yet it seemed to me to throw no light, for the atmosphere round it was always observed to be dark, although the object appeared to us bright. Is the light, then, communicated by the lightning, or is it an ocular deception? We should like to see this strange appearance more fully explained.

From the Dog's Head, hoisting up sail, we soon reached a place called the Loon Straits, where a cluster of islands destroys the appearance of the lake, which is here divided into two leading channels; one of them, running in a south-easterly direction, points out the line of communication for Montreal through the great chain of lakes; the other, to the south-west, directs the traveller to Red River. From the Loon Straits, where there is a good harbour, we crossed over to Grindstone Point, on the west shore; so named from the quality of the stones found there. These stones, although inferior to those imported from home, are, nevertheless, considered a good substitute, and are frequently used: their cheapness recommends them. At this place the character of the rocks seemed to change: instead of the granite found on the east side, freestone, limestone, large flag-stones hard as flint, and others friable, occupy the west side. This place is very rocky, and much exposed to a heavy swell. While we put on shore to breakfast, one of the hands related that soon after he came to the country, the boat in which he had taken a passage started from the Loon Straits in the night, and having a sail-wind, some of the hands lay down on the boat to sleep; on arriving at the point, however, they put on shore for breakfast. Here, one of the men not answering to his name when called, the others, thinking he was still asleep in the boat, went to throw some water on him to waken him; it was then discovered that the unfortunate fellow had fallen overboard during the passage, and was drowned.

Leaving Grindstone Point, a place destitute of harbour or shelter, we continued our course along the west side of the lake, which is thickly wooded with spruce and red pine. Passing the grassy narrows, we reached the sand-bar, which runs obliquely almost across this arm of the lake. Drunken River follows next: this is a small, insignificant creek, deriving a notoriety from being the spot where, some years ago, a carousing party of voyageurs revelled until they were all drunk; hence the name. At Willow Island we passed the last harbour to be found on this end of the lake; ten miles from which is the mouth of Red River, at the southern extremity of the lake.

Lake Winipeg is estimated to be three hundred miles long and about thirty-five broad in the widest place. It lies nearly in the direction of north and south; the water is rather dark and muddy, and although generally shoal, and somewhat dangerous, yet sufficiently deep and navigable for good-sized schooners. The character of the shore is low, barren and rocky, without anything peculiar in its general appearance. During the winter it freezes, and is seldom clear of ice before the 10th of June. The principal feeders are the Great Saskatchewan and Winipeg; but four or five other rivers of considerable size enter it: namely, Poplar River and Beren's River on the east, Swan River and the Little Saskatchewan on the west, and Red River on the south. Squalls and cross currents of air are frequent, and it requires expert hands, as well as a skilful pilot, to navigate it in safety. Canoes are said to be preferable to boats, as almost any place affords them shelter; but I should decidedly give the preference to boats. When the wind is favourable, boats have been known to run from one end of the lake to the other in two days and two nights; but a week is considered a fair passage, although it took us eighteen days. It not unfrequently happens that boats have been detained in it twenty days, according to the state of the wind and weather.

At sun-rise on the 2nd of July, 1825, we made the entrance of the river, which has an insignificant appearance. Its breadth is about eighty yards, current moderate, and the water rather of a dark reddish hue, although it enters the lake over a bed of pure sand. A little distance from the lake, we found two or three families in their nomade condition, living in two wretched huts made of reeds and bits of bark; they were engaged in fishing, and we purchased two fine sturgeon for a cotton handkerchief each. These Indians, a mixture of the Saulteaux and Cree nation, had picked up a few words of broken French and English, by which they made themselves easily understood. They were clever at traffic, intelligent and obliging.

One of them, who passed for the chief's son, harangued us at some length. "My father," said he, "is above," pointing with his hand up the river: "I am sorry he is not here to speak to you. We are but few people, not more than sixty or seventy persons. We are dispersed for the purpose of living. Animals of the chase are very scarce, and the buffalo have deserted our lands.—The white people," said he again, pointing up the river, "are very numerous. They have frightened the wild animals and game from our lands, and have introduced animals and game of their own," alluding to the tame cattle and fowls. "While our buffalo remained, we never prevented the whites from killing them when they were hungry; but they threaten to kill us if we touch their buffalo: we now chiefly live on fish, and they are getting scarce. But although the whites will not let us kill their buffalo nor shoot their game, they are good to us: they give us guns to hunt, they give us thread to fish, tobacco to smoke, and show us how to make roots grow. Our country, once rich, can now no longer feed and clothe us. Look," said he, pointing to the women and children, " look at their garments. They are ragged. Our country is poor; we are no longer independent." The orator then sat down, and taking one of his children up in his arms, began to show us how tattered his clothes were.

We, however, saw nothing very striking in their condition. They seemed to be fat, and as well clothed and thriving as any Indians we had seen. But it is peculiar to some Indians, to plead poverty and to beg. As we proceeded, we came to another little band, where we had a parley with the chief, Pigwise; a short, stout, middle-aged man, with an expressive countenance. He introduced himself to us by showing his medal, and a paper signed by Lord Selkirk, stating him to be a steady friend of the whites. Seigneur Pigwise is not a native of the soil, nor considered an influential chief among his tribe, and owes his chieftainship to the whites alone. Such chiefs are never popular.

So far the surrounding prospect is anything but

inviting, the country being low, flat, and marshy. Having advanced about ten miles up the river, we disembarked on the west bank, and breakfasted on the sturgeon we had purchased from the natives. Breakfast over, we washed, shaved, and brushed ourselves up a little; having, as I thought, entered the confines of a civilised country where we might soon expect to see white men.

We had not been long on shore, before a fellow of mongrel cast emerged from a thicket, driving before him some horses. I immediately accosted him with the view of arranging matters for proceeding on horseback to Fort Garry, the metropolis of the colony; but as the stranger could not speak French or English very intelligibly, we had some difficulty in settling the matter. At last, however, with the assistance of a little Indian jargon, we managed to understand each other, and a bargain was struck; he furnishing me with a good-looking beast, saddle and bridle, for the consideration of five shillings. I then asked him to show me the road, and on his pointing ahead in the direction of the river and assuring me I could not miss it, I ordered the men to proceed with the boat; then mounting my horse, I set off at full speed over a rough surface, covered with willow, poplar, and other obstructions, so that I could scarcely see twenty yards ahead.

My first object was to find the road; but I rode for several miles, and could not find it. As I was wandering to and fro, I met a fellow dressed in red leggings, with a bunch of feathers stuck in his cap, and in his hand a coil of shaganappe, like a Piegan horse-thief. It struck me he must be looking for horses, and I for the road, so we were well met. I asked him about the public road, how far I was from it, and in which direction I should find it. He stopped, stared at me for some time, but made no reply. I repeated the inquiry, asking him again, both in English and French, where was the public road, but with no better success: he remained mute, and we stood looking at each other for some time. Thinking he did not understand the term "public road," I asked him for the road to Fort Garry. "There," said he, pointing his hand before me in the direction of the river, as the other had done before. "Where?" said I, after looking all round and seeing none. "There," said he again, pointing in the same direction. "Where?" resumed I, "I see no road!" "Oh no! there is no road, but we go that way," pointing again in the same direction. Meaning all the time south.

But I was more indebted to the sun than to my guides for pointing out the direction, for had it been a cloudy or dark day, I might have wandered long enough without knowing in what direction I was going, as the word "south" was never once used: a motion of the hand, with the word "There," was all I had to guide me. Seeing I could make no better of it, I set off, and made my way through the bushes; taking care, however, to go as near south as possible. Having advanced about fifteen miles, I stumbled on a sort of road or foot-path, near to a place called the Image Plains, from there being some large stones at the place painted by the natives with images of men and beasts.

At Image Plains the country on the west is open, free from bushes, and, as far as the eye can reach, a boundless prairie. On the east, however, a narrow belt of tall trees running south, points out the direction of the river, and served me as a guide. And here, for the first time, a small herd of tame cattle grazing in the plains attracted my attention, as being the most satisfactory sign I had yet seen of civilisation in Red River. I gazed for some minutes on a scene so novel and interesting, after having been roaming so many years among animals wild as the countries they inhabited. Will these plains, thought I, so long the haunts of the wild buffalo, become the property of the white man? Is not only the red man, but his means of subsistence, to perish before the march of civilisation? While thus musing, I was overtaken by one of the settlers, a very intelligent man of middle age, and as he was riding the same way, we entered into conversation.

My companion and I proceeded, conversing about the present condition and prospects of the colony. He informed me that I was now on the only road that could be called public; though it appeared to me nothing more than a track marked out by the feet of animals, leading at random through the plains, and scarcely visible ten yards ahead of us.

As we journeyed, my fellow-traveller pointed out to me a small isolated dwelling among the trees skirting the river, and looking as if it had no business there. As we advanced, similar buildings, rudely and hastily constructed, became more and more frequent. On asking my comrade from what country the settlers had emigrated, he replied, "From the Highlands of Scotland." In answer to some other queries, he told me that the settlers were pretty comfortable in the land of their adoption; that they paid five shillings for an acre of land, and were exempt from either rent or taxes; that the circulating medium of the colony was printed promissory notes, the highest for twenty shillings, and the lowest for one shilling, sterling, issued by the Honourable Hudson's Bay Company, and answering well enough for every purpose of trade. The government, he said, was solely in the hands of the Company, and was as liberal and indulgent as could be expected; but the market was limited and money scarce, the price of labour high and labourers few.

"There are," said he, "three Roman Catholic priests in the settlement, who have a chapel for their hearers. There is likewise a missionary of the English church, but no congregation; and a Scotch congregation, but no minister! This clergyman, whom, in the absence of one of our own persuasion, we of necessity hear, is a very faithful man in his way; but his ways are not our ways, and because we cannot fall into his views, there is anything but cordiality between us: however, as we have, so far, no choice in the matter, we are content to give him our left hand of fellowship, reserving our right for our own church, whenever, in the course of events, we shall see her walls arise in our land."

My next question he answered by stating, "that there were no towns, nor villages, nor merchants in the colony." I then asked him if there were any magistrates or any gaol; and he replied in the negative. "Then," said I, "you must consider honesty a virtue." He answered me by saying, "There is hardly a lock and key, bolt or bar, on any dwelling-house, barn, or store amongst us, and our windows are parchment without any shutters." "That," said I, "speaks well for the honesty of the inhabitants." In answer to some other questions, he informed me that there were no mills in the colony, nor hardly any attempt at machinery of any sort. With regard to provisions, beef—the principal article of food, there being no sheep in the colony—was two shillings and fourpence per stone, flour twenty shillings per hundredweight, and butter ninepence per pound; while English goods were charged twenty-five per cent. on prime cost.

We had now reached a place called the Frog Plains, and I asked my companion why the place was so named. Pointing to a large swamp in the immediate vicinity, he said, "Because the frogs hold a concert there: formerly the French called it *La Grenouillère*, and from that the English gave it the name it now bears." And here, for the first time, we got a glimpse of the river, sluggishly flowing over its clayey channel, which the work of centuries had gradually scooped out from the level prairie. Here also we saw another small herd of domestic cattle, and some small patches of arable land lying along the banks of the river: for the plough had not yet got beyond the footpath on which we travelled. These patches reminded me of the state of agriculture among the half-civilised natives of the Sandwich Islands, where I have seen a field of moderate size divided into a hundred and twenty plots, belonging to as many proprietors, each cultivating a piece not half the size of that tilled by an Irish labourer for keeping a cow. But these practical indications of labour and industry, as elements of civilisation and moral good, were greatly marred by the continual passing and repassing of armed savages, chanting their war-songs, dangling scalps, and smiling with savage contempt on the slow drudgery of the white man. So that, however flattering were our hopes of Red River, as the source of civilisation and Christianity among the heathen, the results had hardly yet developed themselves.

But we must now glance at the geographical position of the country. Red River, lying in the direction of north and south, has its source at a place called Otter-Tail Lake, near the height of land which divides the waters that run into Hudson's Bay on the north, from those that flow to the Gulf of Mexico on the south. As far as the Grand Forks, a distance of one hundred and fifty miles, it retains its breadth and depth, and is navigable for barges; but beyond that, in many places the water is scarcely deep enough to float an Indian canoe.

If we except about ten miles at the mouth of the river, which is swampy, all the rest, as far as Pembina, in lat. 49° N. (where the boundary line which separates Great Britain from the United States passes), is good soil, rich and well adapted for crops in favourable seasons; yet, generally speaking, the isolated position of the colony, and its northern and frozen locality, almost preclude the inhabitants from intercourse with the rest of the civilised world; except once a year, when the Company's ship from England reaches York Factory. Consequently the remote colony of Red River may be said to be as far from England as any colony or people on the habitable globe. The winters are of seven months' duration, and the mercury freezes.

Neither on the south are its prospects flattering: there the American frontiers skirt the settlement; St. Peter's on the Mississippi being the nearest place of social intercourse with civilised man. Yet the outlet must in the nature of things be south, and not north; though an intercourse with the States cannot be reciprocal, therefore cannot be lasting. An intercourse might indeed prove beneficial to Red River; but Red River by that intercourse can never prove beneficial to the States, it having nothing to give the Americans but what they have got at home. So much, then, for its prospects in time of peace. In the event of a war, however, between England and America, what would be the lot of Red River? It must, without a doubt, be sacrificed. But, apart from the Americans, the Red River settler's greatest dread would arise from the aboriginal hordes that surround him; for although the savages of the north dare not go to the south, or within the American lines, yet the Indians of the south may with great facility travel to the north. All things considered, the only object Lord Selkirk could have had in view by colonising it, was to keep a door open for the fur trade of the far west; and for that purpose it must prove convenient.

Our horses having rested themselves a little, we resumed our travelling. As we journeyed on, my companion and I talked over the affairs of the colony; and from what I had seen, and from the information he gave me, I began seriously to reflect on the choice I had made, and the result was anything but pleasant.

At some distance from the Frog Plains is the Seven Oaks Creek; that fatal spot noticed in a former Chapter,* where the tragedy of the 19th of June, 1816, was enacted. In the immediate vicinity of this, my companion pointed out to me the locality which Lord Selkirk, in a conference with the Scotch emigrants in 1817, had fixed upon as the most convenient site for their church; naming the parish Kildonnan. From Parsonage Creek we advanced through swamps knee-deep in mud and clay. From this position Point Douglas came into view, a projecting tongue of land formed by one of the many bendings of the river, and so named after the noble founder of the colony. About a mile beyond this, is situated, near the confluence of the Assiniboine and the Red River, Fort Garry, the metropolis of the country, and further celebrated as the spot where, in 1811, the Earl of Selkirk concluded a treaty with the Indians for the privilege of settlement. This was the first groundwork of civilisation in this part of British North America. I was anxious to see a place I had heard so much about, but I must confess I felt disappointed. Instead of a place walled and fortified, as I had expected, I saw nothing but a few wooden houses huddled together without palisades, or any regard to taste or even comfort. To this cluster of huts were, however, appended two long bastions in the same style as the other buildings.

These buildings, according to the custom of the country, were used as dwellings and warehouses for

* Chap. III. vol. i. p. 90.

carrying on the trade of the place. Nor was the Governor's residence anything more in its outward appearance than the cottage of a humble farmer, who might be able to spend fifty pounds a year. These, however, were evidences of the settled and tranquil state of the country.

I wished before closing my narrative to have added a few things in reference to the statistics of the settlement; but on this point my companion could give me no information. "No census," he said, "had as yet been taken;" there was, therefore, no document, nor any statement that could be relied on.

Thus ended my first day in Red River; and having, after a somewhat varied and eventful life, settled down, my remarks and my wanderings naturally come to a close together.

THE END.

Woodfall and Kinder, Printers, Angel Court, Skinner Street, London.